Braille Dots. Prison Stripes. Making a Difference

Marie J. Amerson

DEDICATION

Author Natalie Goldberg says in her book *Old Friend from Far Away*, "We write memoir not to remember, not to cling, but to honor and let go."
May this account of my experiences with the prison braille program, this memoir of sorts, be a witness of my time with a special program that made a difference. And, as it allows me to let go, may it honor the men who dedicated their time and their hearts to the Georgia Braille Transcribers.

CONTENTS

ACKNOWLEDGMENTS

I want to acknowledge everyone who was helpful in telling this story about my work with an outstanding prison braille program. Many will go unnamed here, but I hope they know their names are etched in my memory and hold a place in my heart.

I am thankful to the men who took part in Georgia's braille program for demonstrating to me the importance of treating others with respect. My experiences with them also reminded me of other important ways to make a difference in a person's life: recognize one's mistakes and move forward; consider another's point of view; expect others to do the right thing; trust one another; care about the future.

Thank you to Jim Downs, Pat Lehn, and Bill Hinton for their vision of a prison braille program in Georgia and for allowing me to be part of something so great. Zel Murray, thanks for helping those first transcribers learn so much about braille. I appreciate Corrections officers and personnel who kept the "braille lady" safe and made it easy to go to work each day. I was a better prison employee because of these professionals who supported an educator in their midst.

The American Printing House for the Blind employs a wonderful staff of supportive people who understand the role and impact of prison braille programs. I especially appreciate Nancy Lacewell and Becky Snider, Jane Thompson, Jayma Hawkins, Jan Carroll, Gary Mudd, and Bob Brasher for their insights and support through the years.

I want to say a special thank you to early readers Sandy Flatau, Sandy Gilreath, Jim Ferrari for helpful insights, and for your valuable assistance with proofreading, thank you Randy Davis and Patrick Fraser. Any remaining errors are my own fault.

To my husband Jerry, thank you for listening to my frustrations and celebrations, offering warm hugs and steady shoulders to carry me through six years of working in a prison, and for taking the long journey with me to complete this book. ILY!

TO THE READER

Quality braille textbooks do not happen by chance. It takes a lot of work by dedicated individuals so students who read braille can have equal access to educational materials. I wrote this book with three goals in mind: 1) to inform the reader about the process for creating quality braille textbooks for students who are visually impaired; 2) to offer a glimpse into the lives of inmates who commit to performing a valuable service to society by transcribing textbooks into braille; and 3) to encourage readers to balance their perspective of an inmate's past misdeeds with his or her efforts to change.

It is my hope that educators and parents of students who are visually impaired will appreciate the service provided by inmates, and perhaps consider giving ex-offenders the opportunity to continue their work as braille transcribers once they leave prison. I hope prison officials will consider the benefits of offering such a unique program within their facilities and recognize that inmates who commit to the goals of a braille program deserve to be treated with respect and allowed to prove they are different from the general population of inmates.

For more information and guidelines on operating a prison braille program, please contact the National Prison Braille Network at the American Printing House for the Blind in Louisville, Kentucky by calling toll-free 800-223-1839 or visit their website at www.aph.org/pbf/. You can begin your search for additional information about braille by visiting sites such as www.afb.org, www.brailleauthority.org, www.nationalbraille.org, and www.nfb.org.

PROLOGUE

Twenty-four men, each wearing a white uniform trimmed with a dark blue stripe, turned their full attention to a trio of visitors. Not the stiff, military style of attention afforded to officers shouting, "Warden on deck!" These men were listening to a young college sophomore and his former Teacher of the Visually Impaired. The two speakers were somewhat distracted by the din of slamming doors and inmates walking past the window on their way to the barber shop, but the third visitor - a guide dog - took it all in stride. So did the audience.

I had invited *Dustin Johnson*[1]* and *Mary Fitch* to talk to the group of inmates about the importance of braille. The uniformed men were studying to transcribe textbooks into braille and they showed great interest in the young man's description of frustration about encountering mistakes in a braille textbook. The men nodded in apparent agreement when Dustin spoke of the freedom and independence he found by reading on his own, setting his own pace and not having to rely on a sighted person to tell him what was on the page. Inmates smiled when Ms. Fitch, who had worked with Dustin since kindergarten, explained that her former student had not always been an enthusiastic learner.

"But once he learned braille, I couldn't give Dustin enough to read."

The teacher and young college student complimented the men on their work noting the services of braille transcribers reduced the challenges faced in providing Dustin an education. Twenty-four men beamed with pride -- and so did I.

After speaking for forty-five minutes, Dustin and Ms. Fitch answered questions for another thirty minutes. How did Dustin acquire his college texts

---

[1] * Throughout this manuscript, *italics* introduce individuals whose names have been changed.

1

in braille? How helpful were tactile graphics, and how could transcribers make the raised images more useful for a braille reader? What degree was Dustin planning to earn? The men asked Ms. Fitch if teachers of students who are visually impaired prefer to get braille textbooks quickly, or do they want them to be correct.

"Yes!" she said, and clarified that students need accessible textbooks as soon as possible but because they depend on the braille for learning, a textbook filled with errors was worse than having no braille at all. The twenty-four men who worked hard to ensure their work was correct before it left the prison smiled at her answer.

After almost ninety minutes with our group, Dustin and Ms. Fitch seemed more at ease than when they first entered our building after having walked through the prison. Dustin removed his guide dog's harness to allow some of the men to pet Jake, then replaced it so the animal could return to work.

While the men moved on to their next scheduled activity, I located an officer to escort us and walked the quarter mile with Dustin, Jake, and Ms. Fitch to the front gate. Before exiting the final security checkpoint, Ms. Fitch commented on the professionalism and respect she had observed among the inmates in our group. She then thanked me again for the work being done by Georgia Braille Transcribers.

For many of the twenty-four men in the Braille Program at Central State Prison, the ninety minutes Dustin and Ms. Fitch spent delivering a keynote address was the highlight of their two-day Professional Development Workshop. For me, the workshop itself was a highlight of my years with the program. The entire event exemplified the professionalism I had come to know in a most unlikely place - prison.

CHAPTER ONE

In April, 2006, I entered prison as a part-time employee hired to coordinate the Braille Program at Scott State Prison in Milledgeville, Georgia. I came to the position as an educator - not a security professional or counselor or business manager who rose through the ranks as a prison employee. I had spent my career working with young children who had special needs, not teaching adults. And, to be honest, my braille skills were almost completely rusted away because when I retired from the Georgia Academy for the Blind in 2002, I had already been out of the classroom more than half of my twenty-plus years at the school.

I first learned of Georgia's prison braille program in 2004 when my friend Jim Downs, Project Director for the Georgia Instructional Materials Center, announced plans to start the effort in our state. I congratulated Jim on the news, wished him well, and thought nothing more about it as I shed my professional life in the field of blindness.

A year later, Jim shared news about plans to expand the program. He suggested I consider being part of it.

"Oh, I don't think so," I said. "My braille skills have gotten too rusty."

"That's okay," Jim replied. "Men in this program know more braille than you and I will ever know."

I was not convinced at the time, but early in 2006 Jim hosted my first visit to The Braille Cell, the original group of transcribers at Men's State Prison in Milledgeville. Then, he took me a half mile up the road to see space designated for a braille program in Scott State Prison. We met Bill Hinton, Director of Workforce Development for the Georgia Department of Corrections, and though the salary was far less than I could earn in a classroom or as a consulting Teacher of the Visually Impaired, the two men convinced me I had a role to play in Georgia's Prison Braille Program. I liked

3

the part-time, flexible schedule they offered, and I knew the work could make a difference to students who read braille. I accepted the position and embarked on an exciting journey.

CHAPTER TWO

My first full day in prison was a Tuesday, April 4, 2006. I parked outside a fence surrounding three large brick buildings that had once been part of the state's public psychiatric treatment facility. I met my on-site administrative contact, the Deputy Warden of Care & Treatment, who escorted me through security checkpoints and into the administrative offices of Scott State Prison.

After a brief meeting with Warden Rose Williams, who expressed great enthusiasm for the braille program, the Deputy Warden dropped me off in the Personnel Office to complete paperwork, submit to a drug test, and receive other instructions. I was directed to drive around the complex to a different building to be fingerprinted and photographed. Then I returned to the Personnel Office - this time navigating my way through security on my own - where I received my ID badge, a "locator card" which looked much like the ID, and several small brass disks with my name embossed on them. The staff explained I was to wear the ID badge at all times. I would turn in the locator card whenever I entered a building so the prison had an accurate account of the number of people inside the fence in case of emergency. I would submit the brass disks, or "chits," in exchange for a set of keys or tools and retrieve them at the end of the work day when I returned the items to security.

"Other than these official items, it is best to leave everything else outside the fence."

Cell phones were banned. If I wanted to bring in lunch or supplies, I was told to use a clear bag so officers could verify I was not also bringing in weapons or other contraband. The realization hit me that I was going to work inside a fence with glistening razor wire on top; I was limited in my ability to contact the outside world; and, I was considered a possible threat to security. Oh my! Talk about a new work environment.

That's not to suggest Scott State Prison was new. It was not. The 1,700-

bed facility opened in 1981 as one of five state prisons operating on the grounds of the former Central State Hospital and the buildings were showing their age.

From 1842 until the late 1970s and early 1980s, Central State Hospital served as Georgia's main public psychiatric treatment facility. In the latter part of the twentieth century, a few buildings on the 1,750-acre campus continued to house patients with mental illness, and a modern building housed the Georgia War Veterans Home. The hospital grounds - including a paupers' cemetery where former patients were buried - were well-groomed, but some of the oldest buildings had fallen into disrepair and housed only ghosts. As the state transitioned away from using the site for psychiatric services, the Georgia Department of Corrections - the fifth largest prison system in the US - saw an opportunity to re-purpose abandoned buildings. The prison system installed fencing and security gates around buildings that had been constructed in the middle and early part of the 1900s. They transferred employees and inmates to Milledgeville, then began operating several prisons on the grounds of the former hospital.

Though I had never worked in a prison before 2006, I was quite familiar with Central State Hospital. In the mid-1970s, when I completed my studies at the University of Georgia, I joined three other young women to complete a student teaching practicum at the hospital's school. Later, in 1975, I returned to work full time in the special education program that took me onto the wards in various buildings around the hospital. I was familiar with the Holly, Kemper, and Ingram Buildings that now served as Scott State Prison, but I don't recall having entered them during my early teaching career. Back in the 1970s the buildings were not surrounded by razor wire, but on a warm April day more than thirty years later when I made my way through locked gates and doors to enter all three buildings, they were.

The Holly, Kemper, and Ingram buildings that comprised Scott State Prison were spread over a large open tract with no trees. Each building had its own secure entrance, and a wide gate near the administration building allowed motor vehicles to enter the compound to deliver food or equipment. The Kemper and Holly Buildings showed characteristics of circa 1950 or 1960 construction - low red brick with flat roofs. The Ingram Building where I would spend my days with the Braille Program was the oldest. It was built in 1937.

On that first day, once administrative details were complete, I left the Holly Building to walk outside the fence on my way to my work area. I stopped in the parking lot to leave papers in my car and make a brief, calming phone call to my husband. As I sat in my car, I watched an officer at the large vehicle gate use a mirror on a long pole to scan the underside of a food service delivery truck. I noted fifty or so inmates inside the fence walking single-file from one building to another along well-worn paths over bare ground. And I watched a regal red-tailed hawk soar in the bright blue sky high above the prison. Then, leaving everything behind except my chits and ID badges, I locked the car, took a deep breath, and walked to a gate in front of the Ingram Building.

I pushed a large red button by the gate, and as I waited, I studied the exterior of a familiar three-story brick building. I remembered driving by the Ingram Building in the 1970s when I worked with the hospital's education program. Now, though, the structure wore an even thicker layer of glossy white paint and the large windows that let in cooling breezes had been retrofitted to allow light and air to enter but narrowed to prevent a person from squeezing his way out. Screening on the open-air porches that flanked the ends of each floor had been replaced with heavy metal grates.

I jumped when a noisy buzzer sounded and the heavy lock disengaged. I pulled the chain link gate open to step into the first "sally port." (A sally port is a secure entryway controlled by personnel who monitor the space between two doors or gates and operate the locks.) I jumped again when the gate clattered shut and locked behind me then fidgeted until another buzzer sounded to signal it was time to push open the next gate.

After clearing the outside sally port, I walked a short distance to the building where I waited for a lock to disengage so I could open the heavy door. There I found the second sally port with an officer sitting inside a locked booth. She asked my name and business, and upon learning I was the new Braille Program coordinator, the officer instructed me to set my car keys and metal chits on the table outside her window so I could pass through a metal detector. When I cleared that, she asked for my locator card and a chit so she could hand me the ring of keys that would open doors for me to make my way to the Braille Program area. The officer released the lock on the door in front of me and bid me farewell, so I stepped through to a large empty room. The slamming door echoed and fluorescent light bounced off polished floors in the bright cavernous room.

I was on my own. In prison.

The room, thankfully, was populated only with three rows of empty fiberglass benches and machines filled with expensive soft drinks and snacks. I surveyed the doors, including one for an elevator, before locating the entry I needed crowded next to the drink machines on my left. Keys jangled as I found the correct one to unlock the door to a stairway. I stepped through and remembered to lock the door behind me. I was relieved to have the space all to myself as I climbed stairs to the second floor. The control booth officer had explained I would use the same key for both doors I needed in the stairway. I spotted the kitchen on my left (where my key would not work because I was not authorized to open that area) and opened the door to my right to step into another eerily empty room. I thought about the history of the Ingram Building and wondered if the spirit of past residents might still linger. Then, as I considered that current residents might pose a greater danger, I was relieved to see a large man in a crisp blue uniform come around the corner at the other end of the long room.

The tall, dark man greeted me with a warm smile and a firm handshake. Officer Johnnie Foston was in charge of monitoring vocational programs in the Ingram Building at Scott State Prison. It was his domain, he knew everyone who had business in his area, and he was expecting me.

As we walked toward my office, Officer Foston explained the spaces we passed through. He had an easy smile and his deep voice echoed through the work space assigned to the Electrical Training Program. He explained they were out for the day as he showed me workstations where inmates practiced connecting wires and switches as they learned a new trade. The officer pulled a set of keys from his belt and opened a door to show me the tool room, explaining that when the Braille Program needed tools such as scissors or other equipment, I would trade one of my chits for him to hang in place of the outlined tool. It was the protocol to account for a potentially dangerous item missing from its designated spot in the room.

Officer Foston pointed out the staff bathroom across the hall and identified which of the keys on my ring would open the door. He showed me his office, and then two doors down, my own office before helping me open double doors at the end of the hall. As he turned on lights, Officer Foston explained that in the weeks prior to my first day, inmates had set up the training area for the Braille Program. He complimented the professional office appearance of the room, noting how different it was than many areas in the prison. Sensing my nervousness, Officer Foston offered a few words of advice, words that stayed with me throughout my career in prison.

"Mrs. Amerson, I know these men in your program. I know most of them well. Inmates may not want to be in prison, but these men want to be in a program like this. They understand it's an honor and won't likely do anything to mess that up. They won't let anyone else mess it up, either. But - remember this is a prison."

It was the best orientation I could have. Relax, but be mindful. Trust, but don't be gullible. Pay attention and let the work be my focus.

We returned to my office where Officer Foston left me alone with the comforting reminder that he was just down the hall.

I sat at the desk and immediately checked the phone for a dial tone. Ahh - a connection to the outside world! I turned on the computer to determine if it had office software I would need. I knew the computer was not yet connected to the Internet; that would come later. As I shifted things around for a comfortable fit, I did so with the thought that I needed to always secure my phone and computer so inmates could not have access to the outside communication I found so comforting. And, considering my comfort, I realized I did not want to have my back to the door, but I also did not want to feel trapped behind my desk. So much to figure out! So much to remember!

I have no doubt Officer Foston heard me close the door to my office and walk back through the program area as I surveyed it on my own. The large room occupied the entire southwest corner of the Ingram Building's second floor. It was brightly lit, and like other areas in the prison, the concrete floors wore a shimmering coat of wax. Desks were arranged to avoid blocking a path marked in the floor with a yellow line. The route designated where inmates were expected to walk or stand at attention. Some desks were set up next to the narrow windows and others surrounded the four columns supporting the two floors above us. Each was neat as a pin, some with computers and others with a boxy Perkins braillewriter. And, ten desks sported a card with an individual's name.

Once I felt I had a grasp on the new surroundings, I asked Officer Foston to call for the inmates who had been assigned to the program. He noted it was almost time for lunch so we would have to wait until after "count cleared." It was my first lesson about a critically important security routine in prison.

Several times each day - every day of the week, every week, every month - officers count inmates in their assigned areas. The count is reported to a prison official at the designated time each day, and until the official verifies the numbers are correct, no inmate movement is allowed. If an inmate is assigned to a vocational area or has a medical callout and is not on the dorm, he has to remain in that location until count clears. Any discrepancy between the reported count and the number of inmates who should be present results in re-counts until the official verifies all inmates are accounted for. A discrepancy may be a simple matter of someone sloppily writing a number or adding figures wrong, but the process is an important reminder to staff and inmates that a prison is accountable for the whereabouts of prisoners at all times.

The realization of the importance of these daily counts explained why, when I had discussed my schedule with the Deputy Warden, he suggested I arrive at 7:30 a.m. That would put the men in place in our program area for the 8:00 a.m. count; otherwise it could be 8:30 or 9:00 or some other time before they could move from the dorm to the Braille Program. And, as I learned more about the daily count, I made sure to call it a day well before the 4:00 p.m. count to ensure we didn't have to stay in place waiting for the afternoon count to clear.

Shortly after 1:00 p.m. on that first day, Officer Foston announced count had cleared and asked if I was ready to meet the crew. I had reviewed the list of ten names Bill Hinton and the Deputy Warden for Care & Treatment had selected. They had interviewed several candidates from the 1,000 men housed in the medium-security prison and transferred four inmates from the original Braille Program at Men's State Prison. When I said I was ready, Officer Foston called on his radio to have inmates for the Braille Program report out.

Soon, he escorted a line of men in white uniforms into the hall outside my office. The men stood at attention as the officer introduced me and reminded us he would be two doors down if I needed anything. Then, he boomed the command, "At ease!"

I'm not sure who was less at ease - the inmates or me.

I suggested we sit and talk a while so the men unfolded chairs to form a semicircle in the open space outside my office. They offered to roll the chair out from behind my desk, but I had them set up a folding chair for me as well. I asked the men to introduce themselves and tell me what they knew about the program.

The four inmates who had transferred from Men's took the lead, explaining their knowledge of braille, their certifications, and the work they had done as part of The Braille Cell, the name of their transcribing group. Other inmates confessed they knew little about braille but were anxious to learn. Some told me they had already been studying materials one of the transcribers had in the dorm, and all seemed excited about the possibilities the program offered. Then, it was my turn.

Clearly, I was an unknown entity. I had not transferred from some other position in the Department of Corrections, so the "chain gang" rumor mill didn't have much to go on. Inmates had heard the new program coordinator was a retired teacher, but they knew nothing about my teaching style. They probably wondered, "Will she be a strict disciplinarian, an easy target, or someone who will sit back and let inmates run things for themselves?" The men seated around me leaned forward as I told them about my twenty-plus years at the Georgia Academy for the Blind, how I became especially interested in assuring students had access to braille. I told the inmates my goal for the program was to have it operate much like an efficient business, and I shared my educational philosophy: as students they had the difficult task of learning new concepts - I was there to guide them in doing so. "As long as you are doing your best to learn, I will do my best to answer questions, find answers, provide support. I want you to learn so you can do this important work."

I admitted I had never taught adults, particularly inmates and concluded my remarks with, "I understand you are incarcerated for a reason, but I promise - unless you give me reason to do otherwise, I will always try to treat you with respect. I expect the same in return."

Ten heads nodded to indicate they heard my comments and we ended my first meeting with inmates in the Braille Program. The men folded chairs, careful to not scuff the floor as they re-stacked them by the wall. They strolled back to the training room and settled in.

As each man sat at the desk he had selected during the weeks before, I walked through to practice putting names with faces. I commented that it was very considerate of them to label each workstation with their name, then one inmate explained it was actually a matter of protocol so officers knew who was responsible for the contents of each desk. Much like their limited personal space in the dorm, inmates would be held accountable for anything that turned up in their desks during inspection.

I returned to my office, interrupted occasionally by an inmate asking for supplies or wanting to offer a personal welcome to the prison. At the end of the day, Officer Foston suggested I retrieve all the styluses (a small device used to punch braille dots into card stock), and reminded the inmates that all supplies - highlighters, special pens, note pads - were issued for use in the program. He noted that if such items were found in the dorm or on an inmate outside of the program area, it would be considered an infraction which could result in disciplinary action.

Oh! The reality of working in a prison!

CHAPTER THREE

I found it important, especially in the beginning, to remember my focus was not the fact I worked in a prison - I worked with individuals who could make a difference for students who needed quality braille textbooks. I also needed to remember that everyone did not understand what we were doing or even basic information about how braille was used or created.

Like other Teachers of the Visually Impaired (TVIs), I learned braille so I could help students who are blind learn to read and write. Transcribing textbooks is a bit different. Educators understand a student first learns to read and then reads to learn, so they use a formal organized approach to teach a student to recognize written symbols and their meanings. They also depend on quality textbooks, and the same is true regardless of whether their student uses print, large print, or braille. Visual readers do not have to think about how a page is arranged; they simply read the material and find information as directed by a classroom teacher. The readers (and teachers) expect the text to be correct and easy to find.

But when I worked in Georgia's instructional materials center, I learned such quality materials for braille readers were not always readily available. Many TVIs in local schools spent valuable teaching time (and/or personal time in the evenings or on weekends) transcribing information from textbooks so their students had the braille they needed. The TVIs were not always familiar with formatting guidelines, but they were determined their students would at least be able to join sighted classmates in reading a page from the textbook. After all, since textbook publishers do not provide braille versions of their products, educators must find a way to do so because they are charged with the responsibility of providing accessible textbooks.

The process of translating print pages into braille is time consuming and requires specialized knowledge. Agencies such as the American Printing House for the Blind, Region IV Education Services in Texas, or state

Instructional Materials Centers such as Georgia's GIMC usually take on the task of creating the accessible textbooks and many rely on the services of contractors who are certified braille textbook transcribers.

Transcribers study for months or years to become proficient, and even with software advances, human intervention is critical in ensuring quality braille for students. Transcribers must learn everything they can about the tactile system for reading and writing used by blind people worldwide.

Braille was developed in the early 1800s by Louis Braille, a young Frenchman who was blind. He based his work on a system soldiers used to read messages in the dark. It is an arrangement of six raised dots in a cell two columns wide by three rows high. Sixty-three possible configurations of one to six raised dots can be created in a single braille cell which might represent a letter or number, special letter combinations, short-form words, punctuation, or it may provide information about special typefaces. Rules - determined by the Braille Authority of North America (BANA) - guide a transcriber in determining when and how certain configurations may be combined. BANA considers changing technology and other issues to keep the code up-to-date and keep educators and braille producers informed about any changes to the braille code.

In spite of late twentieth century technological advances that enable computer users to translate words from print to braille in a matter of a few software commands, the complexity of a textbook page - with tables, maps, graphics, number problems, and various little sidebars with extraneous text - requires human intervention. That is where the value of professional braille transcribers becomes apparent. Unlike educators who focus on content, braille transcribers focus on *how* a page of text is laid out. They format all the elements of a page so the text is correct and easy to read, so the student who is blind does not have to think about how the page is arranged.

Men in Georgia's Braille Program came to understand the importance of quality braille, how it provided equal access to information and offered students the freedom to be independent readers and writers. And they understood they had a unique opportunity to learn a valuable skill. They endeavored to become professional braille textbook transcribers, and their efforts helped us explain to others the importance of our work.

CHAPTER FOUR

Learning to match dots in a braille cell to corresponding letters or words is a simple matter of rote learning; understanding concepts related to how braille contractions can or cannot be used is a bit more complex. And, these men who were in prison because they had not followed certain rules of society had to work as part of a team. Rules. Guidelines. Exceptions. Teamwork. For some, these were not easy concepts.

To be considered for the Braille Program, inmates had to have a high school diploma or GED, and they had to demonstrate at least an eighth grade reading level on vocational testing to ensure they had the cognitive skills needed to understand course materials. On my first day in prison, four inmates knew braille; the other six claimed they were ready to learn. Some would find the program challenged them in unexpected ways, but it was a challenge all embraced in spite of any fears of failure.

Georgia's Braille Program followed a course of study similar to that of other such programs around the country. We introduced students to a curriculum often used to train prospective TVIs, including me. Also, we required students to use a manual braillewriter while they learned the braille code and basic transcribing rules.

Long before technology opened the door for using a computer keyboard and braille translation software, manual braillewriters were the standard for creating hard copy braille. The Perkins braillewriter is a heavy metal box that looks much like a manual typewriter of old, except it has fewer keys. The user presses an appropriate combination of six keys to correspond to a braille character, and the machine presses metal pins to emboss the character on heavy paper or light card-stock. The braillewriter also has a space bar, backspace key, and return key. Pressing keys takes some effort, but the exercise allows an individual to develop good motor memory for braille, much like a musician develops with practice on a piano. Of course, the laborious task of creating a page of braille might be doubled if the transcriber makes an error near the bottom and cannot adequately rub out mistakes with their wooden braille eraser.

We also introduced students to another low tech device used by braille readers. The slate and stylus is comparable to having a note pad and pen, and many braille readers consider the duo an essential tool for jotting quick notes. Slates, which can be small enough for a 3"x5" card or fit a larger sheet of paper, have two parts hinged together: the base with indented braille cells evenly spaced across the line(s); and a guide with braille cell "windows" to match the indented base. The stylus is a small, awl-shaped device with a pointed end. It is used to punch through the guide windows and create the tactile, raised braille dots. Braille readers like the portability of a slate and stylus, and transcribers find it especially useful for adding labels to tactile graphics that cannot be fed through the braillewriter or embosser.

The task of creating braille can be quite tedious, and since the Braille Program operated long hours, we included a variety of elements in the introductory phase to help prevent burnout from too much time pounding on a manual braillewriter. We encouraged men to select books from our small library so they could learn about Louis Braille, Helen Keller, Anne Macy Sullivan, Eric Weihennmayer, and other visually impaired individuals. Veteran members of the program helped new students create flash cards so they could practice reading braille characters, and we provided "bubble sheets" - pages filled with printed lines of open circles in the form of braille cells. The men filled in the appropriate dots on the bubble sheet to practice "writing" braille. New students often took the flash cards and bubble sheets to the dorm to practice on their own time.

By the time an individual completed the set of twelve lessons in the introductory phase of our program, he and I had a good idea of his potential for success in braille.

Next, students moved into a course of study developed for the Library of Congress, National Library Services for the Blind and Physically Handicapped (NLS). The course is administered by the National Federation of the Blind (NFB). We assigned the student a computer with software that allowed him to use designated keys on the standard computer keyboard to enter braille characters just as he had done on the Perkins braillewriter. The monitor showed an image of the braille document, and a student could choose to print the document for proofreading in the dorm. Early lessons in the NLS course cover content the student had already learned, so individuals had time to grow comfortable with the computer, learn file management, and build other basic computer skills if necessary. (At least one of the original ten members of our group had never touched a computer before entering the program.) It could take an individual several weeks to several months to complete the NLS course, depending on several factors including the student's cognitive abilities, the time he was allowed to work on course exercises each week, the amount of independent study he did in addition to class time, and the amount of time it took the grader to return lesson reports. NLS required that exercises be graded by a qualified literary braille transcriber. Since we had someone who fit their criteria, we graded lessons in-house reducing the turnaround time for the reports. The final lesson, though, had to be submitted to NFB for grading. Most individuals completed the course and submitted their final manuscript to NFB within a matter of six to nine months. A longer time frame suggested the individual was, perhaps, having difficulty or was not sufficiently motivated to be a successful braille transcriber.

After a student submitted his manuscript for grading and while we waited for results, he entered the next phase of the Braille Program - helping to transcribe textbooks. We introduced new software which provided a view with both print and braille on the monitor, as well as indicators to note errors with textbook formatting. While he apprenticed with a veteran transcriber to help create portions of a textbook, the student learned shortcut commands and other software features.

The apprentice activity introduced literary braille transcribers to the issue of textbook formatting, an important component of the skill set needed by anyone who wants to transcribe textbooks. The National Braille Association (NBA) offers certification specific to formatting, but whether or not an individual attained that important milestone, we wanted the men to have a solid foundation in the skill. Experience with textbook formatting was also a requirement for those transcribers who sought to earn certification in other specialized braille transcribing areas such as math, music, or foreign language. Our program faced several obstacles in trying to offer the advanced NBA course in formatting: it cost $100 per person; NBA limited the number of students from a prison braille program at any one time; once an individual completed the course, he needed an outside sponsor to pay the $150 or more so he could take an exam; an individual could take as much as eight weeks to complete the exam, during which time, another exam would not be made available. And in 2012, the governing authority for the braille code approved an update to braille textbook guidelines which would necessitate a revision of the course and exam.

Though we did not face the cost factor in signing up transcribers for advanced NLS courses, their protocol for offering Nemeth code for mathematics or music braille limited our efforts to allow students to seek advanced certifications. NFB would assign a grader to only a certain number of individuals in a prison braille program, and the outside graders took several days to several weeks to return each student's lesson report. When it came time to take the certification exam, the limited number of editions of a test necessitated the policy of allowing only two individuals at a time to attempt the process. A student taking the Nemeth code exam could work on the complex task for up to six months; if unsuccessful, he could reattempt the exam within six months, and during that time, that particular edition of the exam was not available to anyone else in the program.

Despite the hurdles, men in the Braille Program took the initiative to learn as much as possible about transcribing textbooks. The inmates who achieved advanced certifications served as team leaders, and they shared what they knew with others to ensure everyone was working toward the same goal. As Jim Downs had suggested when he recruited me to the program, men in Georgia's Braille Program knew braille - and what they didn't know, they sought to learn.

CHAPTER FIVE

Commitment to learning in a structured environment seems to be a new concept for many men and women in prison. Though some inmates have taken secondary level courses or earned a college degree, a sizable portion of the prison population dropped out of high school and earned a GED only after they were incarcerated. They have enough reminders of past failures and many do not want to be humbled by a situation that might suggest they are limited in their ability to learn a new skill. Braille is not simple to learn, and for some, the meticulous attention-to-detail required to become a good transcriber makes the task of learning even more difficult.

Even with the potential for failure and the difficulties associated with braille, I found many men in Georgia's prisons looked forward to the challenge of learning braille.

They were enthusiastic about learning, but the idea of receiving criticism from a fellow inmate was another matter. Not only did I not meet the NLS criteria for graders, my braille skills were much too rusty to be an effective grader as men progressed through the course. Once an inmate learned to transcribe books, he also had to follow formatting decisions of a lead transcriber or accept critiques from a proofreader who might have more knowledge or experience with textbooks. *Steven Garmin*, one of the original members of the Braille Program at Men's State Prison, provided an excellent foundation for our grading system. He approached the task with great integrity, reviewing each exercise and using the same report model NLS graders assigned by NFB used: review an exercise and note which lines on a page contain an error, but do not cite the specific error on the student's copy; direct the student to resubmit an entire lesson if he misses material for a score of 80 or less; provide feedback in a way that pushes the student to find answers on his own.

Our grading model helped prepare students for the type of reports they could expect when we submitted their manuscripts for final grading by NFB graders or for working with outside graders on advanced courses. Sometimes, Steven explained the type of error so a student could review certain rules before attempting the exercise again, and he maintained a record of all submissions for me to review with him. Usually, the second (and sometimes, third) submission was correct, but ongoing errors suggested a student might need extra practice.

Typically, if an individual was not making progress or other issues arose, Steven offered suggestions about a resolution, but I was the one to discuss our concerns with the student and make decisions about a course of action. Very soon after starting, students came to realize their fellow inmate was not in charge of their fate. They also understood they had to accept his critique. I think it may have helped some of the men when they realized I, too, had to rely on Steven's lesson reports as I studied braille transcribing. Together, we all learned to trust the grading process.

Years after the fact, I learned of at least one occasion when a student objected to Steven's method of grading. The inmate had overlooked a portion of an exercise when he submitted his lesson for grading and was appalled to receive a low, failing grade. The individual was upset that a simple mistake might suggest he was not learning or not serious about braille when, in reality, he was very dedicated to the task.

A few students were not so dedicated, especially in the beginning. Some may have feared the possibility of demonstrating failure, and others were simply slow braille learners. I was disappointed when a few men used whatever means possible to achieve a high grade, but I understood they may have thought anything less would result in immediate dismissal from the program. I tried to reinforce to them my philosophy was more focused on what they were learning; it was not all about the grade.

Whenever Steven or another grader alerted me to a student who was having difficulty with the course, and especially when a student seemed to be taking the wrong path to achieving a high grade, I invited the inmate into my office for a chat. Yikes! It must have felt like being called to the principal's office, particularly for young offenders who were not long out of high school.

I remember one such conversation with *Peter Curtis*, a shy young man who was especially timid around me. Since we required participants to have served five years before entering our program, the barely 21-year-old inmate had not graduated from high school when he entered prison. Peter had earned a GED, his vocational scores indicated an adequate reading level, and fellow inmates in the Braille Program suggested he was smart and would be a good member of the team. He fit in with the group and seemed to appreciate the perks of being part of our elite detail. When the grader noted that Peter had suddenly submitted two perfect exercises after consistently demonstrating difficulty with all the previous lessons, I called the young man into my office.

Peter avoided eye contact as he sat and watched a spot on the floor. I asked how he felt he was doing in the course, and speaking in a voice so soft I could barely hear, Peter told me he was working hard to keep his grades up. Bingo! The comment opened the door for me to explain I was more interested in whether he understood the content of the lessons. I pulled an extra practice page from my set of course materials and asked him to explain pertinent braille concepts from a recent lesson he had completed. As he stumbled over answers I considered he might be nervous trying to spontaneously express himself to me so I suggested he review the relevant lesson and we would meet later so he could complete the exercise with me. I emphasized how each braille lesson laid the groundwork for rules and concepts presented in the next. Then, I reminded Peter he had discretion about when to submit exercises and suggested he slow his pace a bit to ensure he understood one lesson before proceeding to the next.

Peter seemed surprised I did not threaten him with removal from the program because of bad grades and that I did not accuse him of cheating to earn his recent perfect scores. I wanted the young inmate to understand my goal was for him to succeed. I suggested he practice more, focus less on the grade. Then, I said, "Learning braille is easiest for those who really enjoy it. Having difficulty does not mean a person is not smart; it just means he is not into learning braille."

I ended the meeting with Peter by scheduling another the following week. We would review his work and discuss his feelings about being in the program. I directed Peter to find someone in the program with whom he was comfortable and ask that person to be his mentor, someone who would not be responsible for reporting his progress to me. "Someone," I stressed, "who will help you understand braille - not do the work for you."

The conversation was familiar. Before Peter, I had said much the same thing to others. *Joshua Walker. Roger Deaton. Paul Young.* Men who later became leaders in the Braille Program. I think each one recognized the conversation meant I thought they were not giving their best effort to the work, that perhaps, they were being a bit lazy, or rushing through lessons, or not earning their grades the right way. Each time, though, the men seemed relieved to realize I was willing to overlook grades as long as they were doing their best. They saw that I used grades as a guideline, a way to monitor how they were doing, but I focused on a variety of factors to evaluate their progress.

Roger Deaton told me years later about his reaction to our conversation. It came at a point during his Braille Program experience when he realized his life could be different. Roger had listened to my discussion about the commitment required to learn braille, about how he was responsible for making wise use of his time in the program - this, after nine months in the program when Roger had gotten through barely half of the course. He was a busy person. In addition to the Braille Program, Roger participated in various other prison activities - seminary, Biblical Greek, music, softball. He used his quiet time in the Braille Program area to rest up after a hearty round of exercise or to study some of his other topics of interest. "I was not sure I wanted to continue studying braille," he said.

I recall that I thought Roger was very capable, but I was not sure he was sufficiently interested in braille. When we talked, I asked if he planned to stay in the program once he became certified. He was not sure. Roger said after our conversation he weighed his options and decided the opportunity to help others in such a meaningful way was reason enough to commit his full attention to the Braille Program. Though he maintained connections with the other activities, Roger no longer let them take precedence over his study of braille.

Twenty-five-year-old Joshua Walker came to the program as a seasoned veteran of prison having already served nine years of his life sentence. Before prison, the young man had never held a job, and like Peter Curtis, Joshua often did not fully apply himself to the work we were doing. My colleague Bill Hinton and I both talked to Joshua, expressing confidence he could do better work. His fellow inmates demanded more work and less play, and before long, the young man realized he had an opportunity to do more than simply get by. He saw his time in the Braille Program was important, not only to his personal growth, but for braille readers who would benefit from his work. Joshua became one of the most knowledgeable and serious transcribers in the program, though his ever-present shy smirk suggested he continued to enjoy a prank every now and then.

I wish I could say "the conversation" always turned things around, but sometimes, it was not enough. Some men entered the program without a clear understanding of the commitment required. They never considered the potential impact of braille or how, in the future, the program might provide a way for them to transfer new skills to other job opportunities. A few less-than-motivated individuals pushed the limits until Bill and I dismissed them from the program, or they got into trouble elsewhere in the prison and were removed for disciplinary reasons. As if to prove their intelligence, some inmates stayed just long enough to earn their certificate before requesting some other prison detail. And, at least one man who was six to nine months away from his max-out date requested the opportunity to learn another vocational trade so he felt better prepared to find employment outside of prison.

Those who stayed in spite of the challenges, in spite of the humility they faced when a braille lesson reminded them learning is sometimes difficult, those were the men who found the Braille Program most rewarding. And not just because they learned braille. They learned to accept criticism as a way to improve skills, even when the critique came from a fellow inmate. They learned to trust that one bad grade did not mark them as a failure and the best way to build a solid foundation for a difficult skill was to learn the skill. They learned their peers were happy to help, even if it meant guiding them to answers rather than telling them outright.

Also, the men who stayed with the Braille Program reaped rewards from doing something for someone else. Though not financial rewards or time credits that would reduce their sentence, the program made a difference in their lives. It sounded cliche when applicants cited the reason they wanted to become part of the program was to give back to society. But once inmates understood the impact they had on the lives of braille readers, those who stayed with the program realized it was true - they could make a positive difference to someone else.

Many did not see the difference they were making in their own lives until later.

CHAPTER SIX

Inmates entered our Braille Program after going through a process known as "classification." The Deputy Warden of Care & Treatment, counselors, and other personnel reviewed an inmate's folder to determine what programs or classes he needed in order to prepare for eventual release from prison or the work detail for which he qualified. The committee had to consider the inmate's disciplinary record, educational needs, his parole or max-out date, security clearance, and more. In a facility of more than a thousand inmates, the process was daunting.

Unlike coordinators of other vocational programs and work details, Bill and I interviewed inmates before accepting them into the Braille Program. We welcomed recommendations from counselors, the Deputy Warden, and others, but we had to trust the inmates would grasp the importance of quality braille and be able to fit in as an effective part of a team that created accessible learning materials for school children. Without that trust, we felt the program - and ultimately, braille readers - would suffer. Our selection process may have been part of the reason some inmates from the general population referred to our program as the "Holy Braille" of details.

In addition to conducting the interview, Bill and I considered specific criteria: 1) inmates had to have served five years of their sentence so they were acclimated to prison rules and consequences; 2) they had to have three to five years remaining on their sentence to help them have time to earn advanced certifications, build a portfolio, and strengthen braille transcribing skills that would enable them to work effectively on their own outside of prison; 3) individuals had to have at least a GED and demonstrate an eighth-grade or better reading level; 4) inmates had to be free of recent disciplinary reports; and 5) the classification system had to approve their placement in the Braille Program.

When we recommended an inmate for Braille, it could take one week or several before the classification committee approved. Upon placement in the program, the inmate attended a brief orientation which included the warning that supplies were provided for use in the classroom and security would confiscate pens or markers they found on the inmate outside of the program area and possibly issue a disciplinary report as well.

We then assigned the student to a desk with a Perkins braillewriter, course materials, and supplies. Once we had a sufficient number of computers for veterans and new students alike, we placed the equipment on every desk. We established a protocol to ensure the computers for new students did not allow access to braille software until the appropriate time, but for some who had limited computer skills, it allowed them time and practice so they could become familiar with the technology. Many men had earphones they used in the dorms to listen to music so we allowed them to do the same at their computers. I was fine with them having music, or practicing typing or other computer skills as long as they could relate it to braille. "But," I stressed, "NO GAMES!" We monitored the computers to help ensure the men were following our program rules, and occasionally had to re-direct an inmate from using his time in the program to type letters or prepare legal documents for other inmates. And, yes, I had to remove games from the computers on more than one occasion.

When we introduced the student to his primary grader, he was then let go to start on the first lesson using the braillewriter.

The men seemed to appreciate the business atmosphere of the Braille Program, and they seemed to relish the opportunity to learn something unique. Those who took it to heart showed great dedication, often studying braille on their own time. Beginners took flash cards and bubble sheets to the dorm so they could practice reading and writing braille. Some individuals even began studying on their own while they waited to be assigned to the program, perhaps to demonstrate they were serious about wanting to be part of our group.

Veteran transcribers offered encouragement and support to new students, and they, too, took materials to the dorm to study or proofread at the end of their long day in the program area. Some may have enjoyed learning the content in textbooks they were transcribing, and many chose to study textbook formatting to better understand their work or prepare for studying specialized codes for mathematics or music braille. It seems the challenges presented by braille were a nice change of pace from reading endless library books, avoiding the blare of a television in the dayroom, or dealing with thugs who had not yet adjusted to prison life. It's no wonder inmates sought classification to the "Holy Braille" program.

CHAPTER SEVEN

Serving time in prison is not easy. It is not intended to be. A prison sentence is punishment for a crime, and if I were a victim or victim's relative, that might be all I cared about. The fence, the loss of freedom, confinement twenty-four hours a day, seven days a week, fifty-two weeks a year for years at a time. And if that thought is not enough to deter a person from crime, consider the stress of trying to survive among criminals, dealing with strict security protocols, being institutionalized by a life of monotonous routines.

I faced only a small bit of institutional confinement when I worked in the prison, but I carried keys and was free to leave at the end of the day. Even so, I felt the environment from the moment the gate slammed behind me at the first sally port. It continued throughout the day as I interacted with officers and inmates, and I often thought, "How difficult it must be for a newly incarcerated person to adjust to all this!"

"All this" means living among thugs in crowded living quarters, daily inspections, multiple daily counts, random drug testing. It means lock downs, yard call, store call, mail call, and more.

One of my earliest lessons about prison life involved the daily counts that take precedence over almost any other activity within the prison. Census counts are conducted at 8:00 AM, noon, and 4:00 PM, as well as designated times during the evening. No inmate movement between areas is allowed during count because the prison must confirm every inmate's location multiple times during every 24-hour period. The task for stressed-out employees counting more than a thousand inmates and making sure the right figures are recorded is not always simple, so the strict count protocol is necessary to ensure accuracy and security.

Protocol for chow call limits the number of inmates in the dining hall at any given time. The protocol helps stem complications of having too many inmates in the noisy room at once or having members of different gangs interacting with one another, sometimes carrying out grudges. If an inmate eats lunch at 1:00, they might be called to supper at 4:00 and have to bide their time until breakfast at 7:00 the next morning. The inmate must comply with the callout or miss a meal - those are his only options.

Dorm officers schedule yard call to allow inmates off the dorm and into the fresh air. Since it usually occurred during the day, men in the Braille Program missed yard call much of the time. Traveling the compound to and from meals, the program area, or medical callouts was their substitute for yard call unless the men could convince an officer to allow yard call on Friday or during the weekend.

Store call is a highlight to inmates who have money on the books, and mail call brings news from home. Visitation from family and friends is limited to weekends or holidays, and it is strictly monitored. Individual visitors must be cleared in advance, and they must adhere to rules about appropriate clothing and behavior while they sit with an inmate in the crowded visitation room. During the week, and sometimes on weekends, faith-based activities provide respite from time in the dorms. Library call allows an inmate to escape into the world of literature, to research legal steps related to his case, or to spend a few moments visiting with friends from other dorms. Inmates function within such routines because they must.

Protocol and structure are necessary because some prisoners continue to behave as they did on the street, flaunting authority, trying to make deals and please their gang, or behaving in a manner to demonstrate they have power. I, too, had to function within the structure, and I learned to appreciate the routines and protocol that kept me safe.

For instance, an officer escorted me whenever I traveled through the prison, but men in the Braille Program also assured my safety. They did the same for one another, too, because even in our relatively non-violent prison, traveling as a group was as much or more about safety in numbers than a matter of protocol.

I came to understand the safety-in-numbers concept one day at the older, spread-out Scott State Prison when *Bud Harper* was called to the dorm for a scheduled appointment. Bud asked if *Dave Lawson* could accompany him because he needed to stop at the store on his way across the compound. Bud explained if he missed store call because of the appointment, he would not be able to retrieve his items until the following week. "And," he noted, "if I go alone, chances are high I will be mugged before I get to the dorm."

A lone inmate returning from store call could, in fact, be an easy target. Even at Central State Prison, the administration established protocol to deliver store call orders directly to men in their dorms to address the issue of muggings.

As if one could forget the potential for violence in a prison, there is visible evidence it can - and does - take place inside the fence. Men in prison (and women, too, I would guess) have to find balance between being bad-ass enough and getting along with others, between following protocol or orders from officers and maintaining their credibility among fellow inmates. Fraternity or military hazings may have some of the same elements, but initiation into prison life can be daunting. New arrivals are tested by veterans of the prison system; young, immature inmates face bullies asserting their power and status within the prison; small-statured men sometimes feel they must prove they are tough enough to survive; tattoos become more and more elaborate to signal an inmate's allegiance to a particular gang; and when a history of crimes involving children comes out, some inmates face a special wrath from peers. Officers monitor inmates as closely as possible, especially in vulnerable areas, but rape is a real threat.

I came to realize some of the battle scars I saw - missing front teeth or facial scars - may have occurred after the men entered prison. Though inmates can seek medical treatment for injuries, even if plastic surgery was an option, it would have required a transfer to Augusta State Medical Prison, something men in the Braille Program tried to avoid.

It is also possible for a man who angers a fellow inmate to find himself in trouble because of contraband planted to point a finger of guilt his way. Inmates are expected to have their space in order for inspection at all times, and if a cell phone, illegal substance, or weapon turns up in his locker during inspection, officers must take action based on the find.

No matter what else is going on, when an officer shouts, "Warden on deck!" or "Inspection!" inmates must stop to stand at attention with eyes forward and hands by their sides. They must remain in that stance until the warden or officer directs them to be at ease. I never served in the military but imagine the discipline and protocol for inspection must be similar. In prison, though, it serves the additional purpose of helping prison officials manage the tremendous task of providing a secure environment for employees, visitors, and inmates as well as protecting the safety of the general public.

Inspections are meant to control behaviors and ferret out contraband because in spite of their best efforts, officers must contend with drugs, alcohol, weapons, and cell phones. Inmates cozy up to an officer or civilian employee. They offer money. They convince people to smuggle materials into prison or toss it over the fence. They find a way to import contraband and the inspection process is one way of trying to contain the problem.

"Standby for inspection!" signals the beginning of a process that sometimes moves inmates out of a dorm or program area at a moment's notice so officers can search the area. The inmates are escorted to a secure location elsewhere in the prison and held there until the inspection is completed. The CERT team - Correctional Emergency Response Team officers - throw open lockers, turn over mattresses, search through desks, and sometimes, even crawl through the ceiling. They scatter neatly folded clothes, letters from home, and packets of soup. Cell phones and drugs are the more obvious forms of contraband, but something as innocent-seeming as a ball point pen can provide ink for gang tattoos or be sharpened into a shiv, or weapon. Men in the Braille Program occasionally complained about the CERT team's methods, but except for one cell phone incident, the men seemed to avoid major problems because of the intense inspections. They lost a few items (highlighters, sugar packets, etc.) but seemed to understand it was the price they paid for holding onto contraband - anything not approved to be with their personal belongings.

Inmates become accustomed to the loss of privacy and the possibility officers may rifle through their property just as they learn to accept random drug tests or strip searches. If inspection results in the discovery of serious contraband, officers send the suspected offender to "the hole" to await further investigation. (The "hole" is solitary confinement or isolation in a designated area of the prison.) The infraction may result in a disciplinary report (DR), removal from an assigned detail, transfer out to another prison, and sometimes, a formal charge that adds time to an inmate's sentence.

Though I never saw evidence of a cell phone in the Braille Program, one day, as the men lined up to go to lunch, the inspection team stopped them in their tracks just outside my office. Officers patted down each man before allowing him to leave the J-Unit then left without any explanation to me. When the inmates returned from lunch, Bud Harper explained the CERT team was looking for a cell phone because another inmate had implicated someone from Braille. I expressed my hope that the claim was false and Bud assured me he did not have a cell phone in his possession. He may have told the truth, but within a few weeks, a fellow Braille Program participant was sent to the hole because officers caught him with a cell phone in the dorm.

Bill and I had always made it clear to inmates that one criterion for being in the Braille Program included maintaining a record free of DRs. A minor infraction, or a DR investigation that cleared an inmate of wrong-doing did not necessarily warrant the inmate's removal from the program, but a major infraction such as the serious contraband violation did. The inmate charged in the cell phone incident was dismissed from the Braille Program and transferred out of the prison. A year later, the man sent word he wanted to return to the Braille Program. I was reluctant. But Bill - who understood prisoners and the corrections system far better than I- suggested we give the inmate a second chance. We approved the request and notified the warden so, pending administrative approval, the man could return to Central State Prison. When he re-entered the program, the individual focused, once again, on being a positive member of our team.

I was relieved to find that instead of considering our action as being soft with our rules, inmates in the Braille Program seemed to appreciate we were willing to give the offender a second chance. Perhaps the men saw Bill and I accepted they might take a wrong step on their path to doing the right thing, and much like our philosophy about grades, we considered the big picture of their efforts to change. At least, that's how I hope they interpreted our efforts.

Though inspection is a serious matter for inmates and officers, I recall with some amusement my naivety about one aspect.

The CERT team often uses a K-9 officer during inspections. I had noticed inmates give wide berth to visiting guide dogs, and thought, "He must be afraid of being bitten." I sympathized with the idea until it finally dawned on me the bite most inmates feared was if the dog detected drugs or other contraband. Many of the inmates did not recognize the difference between a dog guiding a person who is blind and the dog an officer used to sniff out drugs. Or, perhaps they just didn't trust there was any difference in the animals.

My sense of smell might not be as sensitive as that of a dog trained to detect drugs, but my aversion to cigarette smoke made it easy for me to sniff out tobacco use. When I first started in 2006, smoking was permitted in designated areas of Scott State Prison. As the smokers returned from their breaks, I often held my breath or tried to avoid conversation with the men until the noxious fumes dissipated. Smoke breaks continued to be part of our daily routine when we moved to Central, then in 2010, like most other prisons in the state, it became a tobacco-free environment - at least in theory. Tobacco became another form of contraband, like drugs or cell phones, and it continued to find its way inside. Officers monitoring the dorms might not have noticed (or, chose not to notice something they considered to be a minor infraction), but I could tell when someone in an adjacent dorm was smoking. Inmates from the dorms quickly learned it was no use to try and sneak a smoke in the hallway outside my office because I would call an officer to address the situation.

I learned to adapt to the minor disruptions caused by a general call for inspection to prepare for visitors or the security inspections conducted on the dorms. Sometimes when the CERT team emptied our unit for inspection of the dorms, men from the Braille Program would not be allowed into the building until the inspection was completed so I used the quiet time to work at my desk without the usual interruptions to my train of thought.

When we were at Scott State Prison, I also stayed put in my office when Officer Foston alerted me to security inspections taking place on the hall that served as my primary entry/exit point. It was also the location of the staff bathroom, so if I needed, Officer Foston would escort me out of the area through an alternate exit. He wanted to ensure the security routine was not compromised, but I think he also steered me away from the area to protect my modesty.

Unfortunately, I could not always avoid unpleasant inspection situations. One day, I found myself in the wrong place and witnessed officers berating a young inmate waiting to submit to a strip search and drug test. I had gone to the Security Office in the Ingram Building to use the only copy machine available to me. Before I could finish making copies of a document we were using in the classroom, officers began lining inmates up along the wall between the copy machine and the door, my only way out. One officer stood at the door of the small bathroom and directed an inmate to enter and provide a urine sample while he watched. Two other officers kept other inmates standing at attention along the wall as they waited. Realizing what was happening, I pulled the remaining pages to be copied as quickly as possible and prepared to leave when the machine delivered the last pages in the cue.

I was not quick enough. It seemed one young inmate was not complying appropriately with the officers' expectation for standing at attention. They shouted and he shouted in return as he tried to explain his situation. The young man may have known he would test positive for drugs, but I also wondered if he might be newly incarcerated and had simply not yet learned all the rules and expectations for how to behave in prison. I tried to rationalize the exchange as a necessary way for officers to assert themselves, but the incident that brought the young offender to tears was disconcerting for me to witness. The loud arguing echoed in my head the rest of the day, even after I returned to the relative quiet of the Braille Program.

Unlike security personnel, I did not usually have to assert my power over inmates. If I had a problem with an inmate, whether from the Braille Program or the general population, I could call on an officer to deal with the situation. I knew my role as a civilian employee offered a different perspective on dealing with inmates and I always tried to remember the important role of the officers. They were there to control criminals, and it was not always clear which of the men in white uniforms would jump on any opportunity to misbehave inside prison.

Unfortunately, some prison employees also take the opportunity to engage in criminal behaviors or forget to adhere to the rules governing their employment in a prison. Some get entangled in personal relations with inmates; a few behave in an abusive manner; and others bring in contraband. Every employee who enters a prison gate sees the signs about smuggling illegal substances:

> The Georgia Department of Corrections does not tolerate contraband in any of our facilities. If an employee, volunteer, visitor, or offender in our facilities is found to have or be transporting contraband, they are arrested and prosecuted to the fullest extent of the law.

During my time at Scott and Central State Prisons, I was not aware of incidents of an employee being arrested, but I know it happened at other prisons around the state. Each morning at Central as I traveled through the administration building, I saw the television screen that posted announcements and reminders from the Department of Corrections. The broadcast showed data on the number of recent incidents and included the names of employees arrested for violations. I would always wonder, "What would drive a prison employee to risk so much? Why would they risk becoming an inmate themselves or put fellow employees in danger just to provide tobacco, food, drugs, or worse to a convicted criminal? Do these employees expect they will not get caught?"

They do get caught - employees and visitors, civilian and security personnel, men and women. The following incident from 2013 is just one example noted on the Georgia Department of Corrections website:

> On May 18, 2013 Washington State Prison Officer *Jane Doe* failed to clear the front entrance metal detector. Officer Doe was searched and was found to have the following items on her person: two smart phones and three batteries. In addition, she had four containers of Vodka, two pairs of sunglasses, five cooked steaks with bread and ten packs of candy in a bag. Officer Doe admitted to receiving one thousand on a green dot card (money assigned to a prepaid debit card) to bring in the contraband. Officer Doe was arrested by the Washington County Sheriff's Office.

The penalty for introducing contraband into a Georgia prison can be one to five years in prison, and this woman - one of more than 100 employees who have been arrested for the crime over the past few years - destroyed her future for someone to put $1,000 on a prepaid debit card! In July, 2014, after admitting to smuggling in alcoholic beverage mix, cell phones and batteries, cigars, and various other items, Officer Doe was criminally charged with a string of felonies. The former corrections officer was sentenced to serve five years of a twenty year sentence.

As difficult as it is for me to understand the motivations of such an officer, her arrest and conviction highlight the situation for many inmates - they make bad decisions or act in a moment of passion without thinking of the consequences. As one former participant in the prison braille program in Arkansas wrote in a book about his life as a drug user, inmate, and ex-offender, "I did not set out to hurt my mama or rob my friend or do anything wrong. All I cared about was getting high."

The man served time - several times - and it took a true change of heart for him to realize his actions affected others. He (and perhaps the officer who smuggled in contraband) landed in prison, an institution serving bland meals prepared on a budget; he wore a uniform and became a number. He found himself being counted and monitored and inspected each and every day while trying to avoid injury or worse from fellow criminals. He was confined every day to a space defined by razor wire. He lived the prison life.

Indeed, how could one ever adjust?

CHAPTER EIGHT

Living the prison life means facing predictable routines, but change and unpredictability are also factors. Inmates face the possibility of being transferred to a different facility because of security issues, so they can access programs to prepare them for release, or simply to facilitate administrative issues associated with trying to house new prisoners entering the system. Georgia's prison system is one of the largest in the United States. The Department of Corrections operates and maintains more than thirty facilities, and some of the compounds quickly fall into disrepair because of the use and abuse of nearly 60,000 men and women confined within their walls.

When I started with the Braille Program in 2006, Scott State Prison was already showing its age. The buildings had been part of the state's psychiatric hospital before it was turned over to the Department of Corrections in 1981. The newest structure at Scott had been built circa 1960, and the Ingram Building where we operated the Braille Program had been constructed in 1937. We heard rumors about the prison closing and on July 7, 2009, Bill and I received official word that Scott State Prison would close in less than six weeks.

The Department of Corrections was well-prepared for the announcement; Bill and I were less so even though we had expected the move for a while. My colleague and I were uncertain what effect the closure would have on the Braille Program, and the two of us suddenly had to face tough questions from the men we worked with each day: Where will the program go? Would the department transfer all inmates in the program to the new location? How would any such move impact travel times for inmates' visitors? Would the Braille Program close?

Bill and I answered each of their questions with a tentative confidence and a few, "We don't knows." We assured the inmates the Georgia Department of Corrections valued the Braille Program and would not allow it to end simply because Scott State Prison was closing. Then, as the inmates returned to their desks to fret and prepare for the big change, Bill and I closed the office door and asked each other, "What is going to happen?"

Perhaps I was more uncertain than Bill. After all, he was a veteran of Georgia's prison administrative system, a former warden and program administrator. He set to work right away and started laying the groundwork for a successful transition. He called officials at the regional and state level and reminded them about the important work the Braille Program was doing. He explained the importance of having knowledgeable inmates in the program and asked the officials to consider transferring as many current program participants as possible to our new location. He asked for recommendations about potential sites for the program and suggested something close to Macon might work best. Within days of the announcement about the prison closing, I had regained my own confidence about the future of Georgia's Braille Program.

A week after the announcement, Bill and I met Bill Terry, the man assigned to become the new warden at Central State Prison in Macon. The medium security facility constructed in 1978 housed 1,000 inmates, and except for the double layer of razor wire-topped fence, the compound looked much like a nearby college campus. Seven living units dotted the rolling terrain inside the fence. The large two-story Administration Building we entered after moving through two sally ports also contained a dining hall, medical offices, education programs, and security office. Our group - including the warden, a cadre of officers and other personnel, Bill and me - walked past the security office where a path led to the gymnasium. I noted, in spite of the lack of trees, a pleasing landscape with neat beds of zinnias, roses, and other flowers in spots all along the walkway. We passed a small goldfish pond and the warden explained the miniature mill with a waterwheel had been crafted by inmates in the carpentry class.

Warden Terry led the way to show us space in the gymnasium he thought might work for the Braille Program. Bill and I looked at each other with dismay. The space was small, and we felt activities in the gym would be too noisy and distracting for the kind of work we did in Braille. Warden Terry and his staff offered an alternative. As we left the gymnasium, I was concerned he might take us to the Correctional Industries Garment Manufacturer next door. It was a work facility enclosed within a separate fenced area of Central State Prison. I had visited the facility in the past and appreciated the large work area, but did not think it would work to share space with the other program. I was relieved when the warden and his group led us around the opposite corner of the gymnasium.

We went to the J-Unit, a "fast-track" building that housed inmates in four large open dormitories. As we traveled down the hill, the warden noted the prison laundry beyond the dormitory, and pointed out several buildings outside the fence: a warehouse, maintenance shed, and space designated for staff training. I noticed cameras mounted high on the fence or on building corners, and noticed the "P-car" (perimeter patrol car) cruising along a road just outside the fence.

J-Unit was not like most of the living units at Central. Dormitories up the hill near the center of the compound each housed ninety-six inmates within four pods. An officer inside a small office allowed inmates through a gate into a central courtyard and then into their respective two-story pod. Each level in a pod had six small two-man rooms and shower facilities for the twelve men on the hall. From the office by the unit gate, the officer monitored camera views of each dorm's dayroom or upper and lower halls as well as the unit's courtyard.

By contrast, J-Unit held 288 inmates in four open dormitories. An officer sat or stood outside the doors of two rooms on each side of the large central hallway to control traffic in and out of the day rooms and monitor dormitory areas visible through large windows. Another officer sat inside a secure, slightly elevated control room and monitored camera views and controlled the main points of entry into the building. Except for the large shower and bathroom, the only open space in each dorm was the dayroom with a loud television secured to one wall. Inmates gathered at tables with attached seating or occasionally made calls on the pay-phone hanging near the windows overlooking the interior hall. Thirty-six double bunk beds and seventy-two lockers lined the walls of the sleeping areas. (In 2011, Central State Prison received more inmates as the Department of Corrections realigned facilities, so a third bunk was added to the array and an additional thirty-six lockers took up space in the day room.)

The original purpose of J-Unit as a fast-track facility meant it was designed to function as a stand-alone part of the prison. The building included a dining room and kitchen in a hallway separated from the dorms by a set of locked doors. By 2009, the large space was being used only for storage, and that was the area Warden Terry and his staff took us. Bill and I imagined the large open dining room full of desks and the kitchen space filled with production equipment. The sergeant opened a door across the hall that showed potential for our office and secure storage space for supplies and extra equipment.

Within days, department officials approved the plan to move us, so Central State Prison staff set about refurbishing the space to meet our needs. They installed carpet to help reduce noise and added electrical lines to handle the computers and equipment we would bring.

For braille transcribers, July and August are the busiest months of the year. They are transcribing and producing books for a new school year. We received the news about our move on July 7, 2009: Scott would close and be empty no later than August 15. Though we were relieved to know where the program would go, all of us were concerned about trying to complete textbook assignments amidst the confusion of preparing to move. Inmates coordinated their efforts so some packed reference materials and others held theirs out until the last minute in case someone needed to look up a formatting rule. They did the same with supplies and equipment. As they worked on twenty-five textbooks assigned for the new school year, the men held off disconnecting computers and securing braille production equipment until the last possible moment. By the close of business on July 28, the Braille Program delivered at least the first volume of every textbook to GIMC. Subsequent volumes would have to wait until we got settled, but the men were determined students would have the first portion of their textbooks when they arrived at school in early August.

A week later, on August 4, I entered Central State Prison for my first day of work there. Having worked in a prison for more than two years already, I was accustomed to the security protocol and prison environment. I was not as nervous as I had been for my first day at Scott and found it much easier to focus on the task at hand - directing where to put various items as inmates unloaded a large semi stacked high with twenty-five workstations, chairs, computers, boxes of supplies and materials, braille production equipment, and more. Dorms were locked down and Security staff supervised as inmates removed a portion of the razor wire at the back of J-Unit so the inmates learning to drive a big rig could back the truck down to a loading dock at the back of the building. Central State Prison assigned a crew of inmates to unload the truck because Braille Program inmates were still in the process of transferring from Scott. Though I was confident the staff had selected inmates they could trust with the task, I was worried as inmates lowered the large braille embosser and other expensive technology off the truck. I was concerned they might not handle the valuable equipment with the same care inmates from the Braille Program had used when they loaded the vehicle in Milledgeville. I was less concerned about the desks, chairs, and boxes the men stacked in the former dining room and kitchen.

Everyone - Department of Corrections officials, Central State Prison administrators, GIMC, the braille transcribers - made a tremendous effort to minimize any disruption our move might create for students who required the accessible textbooks we were creating. Braille Program inmates were among the first transferred out of Scott and most were transferred directly to Macon without having to spend a week or more in some transitional placement in another part of the state. By August 11, one week after I watched the truck being unloaded and two weeks after I spent my last day at Scott State Prison, most inmates from the Braille Program had completed the transfer to Central. Protocol usually required new inmates in a facility to attend orientation and go through the classification process before being allowed off the dorm to go to a program area, but Warden Terry approved an exception so the men could start setting things up as soon as possible. By the end of the second week of August, I delivered more volumes of the braille textbooks students needed as they proceeded through the school year.

Bill, the inmates, and I settled into our new environment. I was delighted to have a shorter commute but sympathized with Bill who now had the forty-minute drive each way. Even the men in the program had a shorter "commute" during their first six months at Central.

Inmates in the Braille Program awoke each morning in the noisy open dorms of J-Unit. They traveled up the hill to the dining hall for breakfast, then returned to J to watch for Bill or me to pass the window of their dorm. Once the officer released them, the men walked less than twenty feet and passed through doors into the "Holy Braille" area. Except for lunch or a smoke break, the men spent their entire day in our area before returning to the dorm at the end of the day. Sometimes, the men persuaded an officer to allow them a few extra minutes on the yard or they got permission to visit the library so they could capture a bit of time outside the confines of the noisy J-Unit.

As soon as we thought it prudent, Bill and I lobbied for the men to be placed in a different living unit. We explained the quieter setting would allow them more opportunity to study or proofread braille in the evenings, and we noted it could be a small reward for the diligent work the men did for children in Georgia's schools. Warden Terry established one 24-man pod as the Braille Unit so men in the program could continue to work and study together in the evenings. Each man received a key to the room he shared with another transcriber, and though officers or the CERT team could enter the rooms any time, the key was a powerful status symbol to many of the men. More importantly, though, the men seemed relieved to spend their evenings in a quieter environment and appreciated their opportunity to have a slightly longer commute.

The inmates' move to a dorm up the hill provided an unexpected benefit for me as well. Their new quarters in the E-Unit placed the Braille Program inmates in a position to watch for me to exit the Administration Building door where I entered the compound each morning. I often carried in books or supplies and left with volumes of braille textbooks in the afternoon, so their proximity made it easier for the men to help carry the load. But I also appreciated their new location for another reason.

Having to take the long walk through the compound at Central meant I spent more time around inmates from the general population than I had at Scott. During winter months, I arrived at the prison before daylight, and since security protocol directed me to have an officer escort me to J-Unit, I sometimes had to walk past inmates waiting for pill call or trailing their way to the dining hall before I found an available officer. Yes, the area was monitored by cameras, but I was uneasy walking alone the twenty yards to the Security Office. With their move to E-Unit, Braille Program inmates kept watch for my arrival, so even if I had to wait outside on the walkway while Security called an officer from J-Unit to come up the hill to escort me or find an officer who was not too busy to escort me, I knew the braille transcribers were watching out for my safety. One or more of them would stand with me as an officer finished paperwork or received clearance to leave his post to walk with me down the hill.

The walk to J-Unit was easy enough until we turned the corner at the gym. The narrow sidewalk, bordered on each side with tall chain link fence, dipped sharply just beyond an area where the prison was adding another large open dormitory. Ankle-twisting trenches marked the edges of the 36-inch wide walkway where it took a second sharp dip at the corner of the J-Unit. Going downhill was one thing, but the afternoon trek back up the hill - often with boxes of braille books - was almost as bad for us as it was for inmates rolling large carts full from the laundry that sat just beyond our building.

Because access to the laundry facility was limited, there was a gate to the area at the intersection where we entered J-Unit. We had to wait for the control officer inside to unlock the red door for us to enter. It was another spot for inmates to gather, and another area where I sometimes felt uneasy. Once inside, the men and I passed the control booth and the dorms they once occupied before opening doors to our relatively isolated portion of the building.

As we settled into the new environment of Central State Prison, I had other adjustments to make as well. I missed the comforting presence of Officer Foston. Because our program was located far from other vocational programs, we did not have an officer assigned to manage the daily count, inmate callouts, or to monitor general traffic in our area. The unit's sergeant and officers would add that responsibility to their busy schedule.

In spite of signs posted to direct inmates to wait outside the doors that separated our hall from the dormitory areas, men gathered outside the counselor's office next door. If possible, they crowded into the closet-sized barber shop to visit and socialize without the control officer noticing them in the hall. These men from the general population stared through the window into our work area, fascinated by the computers and the fellow inmates sitting at a quiet work task. They quickly forgot how loud voices bounced around in the cinderblock building, and of course, some just didn't care if their noise bothered me or anyone else in the prison. It didn't help that J-Unit officers seemed to tune out noise and activity in our area. I tried to tolerate the situation, but when extra traffic on our hall became too much for me, I would call the control booth or phone the sergeant and ask security to run inmates back to the dorm.

Men in the Braille Program noted my frustration about our noisy setting, and one day Dave Lawson brought me a cartoon from the daily paper: Mom asked the kids, "How was school?" The kids replied "Loud! First we had assembly, then a fire drill, and indoor recess because it was raining. You couldn't hear yourself think." (I especially related to that part.) When the Mom asked her kids how they handled all the noise, the little girl said, "I cover my ears." The little boy glibly replied, "I stop thinking."

I think, at times, I may have responded to our noisy hall the same way.

Among the new routines at Central, the protocol for delivering our daily count changed. Bill and I maintained a roster on our computer so we had the daily noon count ready when the sergeant called for it. The men in the program maintained a sign-in sheet in their work area, and we used it not only to teach about accountability in the work place, but to help us keep track of their whereabouts as well. We reminded the men to notify us when they needed to leave for a callout and when they returned.

Within a year after our arrival at Central State Prison, Warden Terry approved a plan for us to occupy additional space in J-Unit. A prison construction detail built a new wall to separate our office from the cavernous storage space, then they knocked a hole in the wall and framed a new door into the area from the hall behind us. The new configuration included windows in the back wall of our office so we could monitor activity in the new work space which included the hall and space once designated as the unit sergeant's office.

Not so different from my routine at Scott, I usually stayed in my office most of the day. Rather than make the trek to and from the Administration Building when the men went to chow, I had lunch at my desk. When I needed a bathroom break, I secured the office, walked to the end of the hall and pressed a button so the control officer could unlock a door to an outside hallway. If a lot was going on in the building, the control officer sometimes missed hearing the buzzer. If I could catch the attention of a nearby officer, he would call the booth to "Open Door 9," or sometimes inmates on the hall would pass along the message I was trying to leave.

Once permitted through Door 9, I sometimes took the opportunity to step out through another set of doors to admire a small flower bed planted between the building and the large gates of a rarely-used sally port. I would enjoy a few minutes of quiet and solitude broken only by an officer patrolling the perimeter in the P-Car. Then, I returned through the unlocked doors to face the rest of my day in prison. One office on the hallway to the staff restroom was occupied, so I sometimes took the opportunity to chat with the woman who worked there before returning to the noise on our hall. And, as I stood on the outside of Door 9, I again often had to wait for someone to hear the buzzer or for inmates to ask an officer to let me through.

Even as I adjusted to the new location for the Braille Program at Central State Prison I realized, though it might be different from Scott, prison life was much the same no matter the buildings and scenery inside and outside the fence. The people inside were the same.

CHAPTER NINE

I sometimes asked myself, Why work in a prison? Why spend my days inside the fence where noise bounced off cinder block walls, linoleum floors, glass and metal, where inmates shouted to be heard and officers shouted even louder? Why deal with trying to avoid altercations in the hall or foul language roaring out from the dorm next to my office? Why face interactions with officers who expected trouble from everyone and made no effort to recognize when individuals were trying to do better? Why put myself in a position where I had to consider potential threats to my safety?

Whenever the questions arose, I tried to think about my purpose for being there and review a favorite Helen Keller quote:

"More than any other time when I hold a beloved book in my hands
my limitations fall from me, my spirit is free."

Remembering the importance of our work was usually enough to keep me going. As for the potential for danger, I soon realized it was not the concern it might have been because in addition to security personnel, inmates from the Braille Program offered their protection to me.

Just as they did when I walked in each morning, men from the Braille Program usually accompanied me any time I trekked through the prison. If the officer escort lagged behind or got distracted along the way, I still felt safe knowing that *Ricky Camden* or Dave Lawson and others were between trouble and me. As Officer Foston had advised on my first day of work, the men did not want anything to happen to make me uncomfortable about being in prison. But, I kept in mind that it was not the inmates' job to protect me. They had to avoid situations that might result in an altercation with other inmates.

I did not recognize the inmate "protection detail" right away even though it was present from the very first day at Scott. There, Officer Foston left his office each day at 3:30 to make rounds and secure the vocational areas of the Ingram Building. He unlocked doors to the stairway so inmates from all the programs could leave in time to be back on their dorms for the 4:00 count. Officer Foston returned to the second floor in time to bid me goodbye and ensure all the vocational program inmates had gone before he sat at his desk to complete paperwork.

The men in our program knew to wrap up their day by 3:30, but occasionally one might be delayed. When that happened, I always asked Ricky or Steven Garmin or others to stay behind so I was not alone with any one inmate. I did not expect trouble; I was being cautious because I wanted to ensure there was never a question of safety or impropriety. It never occurred to me that the men, too, considered it best practice to have more than one stay behind.

One day, I specifically asked Ricky to stay until *Matthew Stevens* finished at his desk. Ricky, who was quiet and timid, surprised me with his frank response. He assured me he and his peers always made sure Stevens was never left behind where he might find me vulnerable. They didn't trust the inmate because they knew his history, and they were concerned for my safety.

The protection detail addressed a similar problem after we moved to Central State Prison. The J-Unit sergeant allowed the orderly for his unit free reign to move around the building so he could keep floors and walls sparkling clean for inspection. The orderly often stood outside my office when he had nothing else to do, and naive me, I thought he positioned himself there to be ready in case I needed to call for the sergeant or send for one of the transcribers across the hall. Dave Lawson had positioned his desk in front of the wall of windows in their workspace across from my office so he could monitor the hallway outside, including my office. One day, Dave and other men in the Braille Program caught sight of the orderly masturbating as he stood peering through my office window. A few men stayed behind during chow call, at least until the orderly left to go to lunch. Then, as soon as possible, the men spoke to Bill about the incident. The orderly was transferred to a different housing unit right away, and the next day that I worked, Bill called with an explanation.

It was disconcerting to hear about the orderly's indiscretion, but I was relieved to know the inmates in the Braille Program and my co-worker watched out for me. And, it served as a reminder of the importance for me to always remember where I worked.

CHAPTER TEN

I worked in a prison. A crowded, noisy, sometimes scary place inside a razor-wire fence. But, I worked with people who cared about others. And, they cared about the important work they were doing.

Certification as a literary braille transcriber indicates an individual knows the braille code, its rules and exceptions, and he or she can produce an almost error-free manuscript from a library book. Creating a braille textbook is more complex, and in spite of technology advances, the task still requires expert human intervention. A transcriber reviews a textbook, researches appropriate rules and examples for braille formatting, interprets graphics, and creates consistent linear pages with all the elements that allow a braille reader to be on par with sighted readers.

For instance: Is a colored font used throughout a textbook as "eye candy" just to add visual interest, or does it serve a particular purpose? Are photographs included to impart information to the reader or to fill space on a page? Graphic elements - photographs or images such as maps, graphs, charts - must be interpreted for the braille reader whenever possible, so transcribers must consider the target reader's age to ensure they use appropriate language tags, i.e., "Ask your teacher for help," or "Photo omitted," or use words the reader can understand to describe a two-dimensional image. Alternately, the transcriber may need to create a three-dimensional representation of the graphic. A transcriber must determine when to use Nemeth code for mathematics and science so the reader understands whether a particular combination of dots represents numbers or letters. A lot of thought goes into interpreting a textbook page for braille readers.

Advanced certifications in braille and a portfolio demonstrating a range of textbook experience help document a transcriber's level of expertise. A long-term commitment such as we expected in our program allows a transcriber to acquire both, and it increases the probability an ex-offender can find work as a braille transcriber when he or she leaves prison. Agencies and organizations responsible for procuring accessible educational materials expect individuals with such documentation can produce quality materials for braille readers.

The Braille Cell, as the transcribers were called at Men's State Prison, started Georgia's Braille Program by transcribing literary materials and advanced to more diverse textbooks as inmates gained skills. In 2007, when the consolidated programs had become known as Georgia Braille Transcribers, GIMC added production capabilities so men in the program could transcribe, create tactile graphics, emboss and assemble textbooks. The move generated greater fiscal savings for the state because every book transcribed and produced by Georgia Braille Transcribers was one less book GIMC had to purchase from an outside source.

A newly transcribed braille textbook can cost anywhere from $1,000 to $15,000 or more because of the cost of transcribing. Subsequent copies of the text will cost much less, but it has to be available as a braille file before it can be produced as a braille book. Currently, transcription costs can range from one dollar per page of braille for a simple book to five dollars per braille page for a math or science book or one that contains a lot of graphics. And, because of its linear format, each printed page in a textbook translates to being about two-and-a-half braille pages.

Consider a 100-page print text in reading or literature. It might not contain many pictures to be interpreted as tactile graphics, so the transcription is a simple process. Still, it would likely result in 250 braille pages contained in two or more separate volumes. The cost for transcribing the book could be $250 with an additional production cost of $100. ($50 for each of two volumes.)

Now, let's make the 100-page print text a math book containing lots of graphs and images that have to be explained. The extra skill required for using Nemeth code adds to the complexity; so do the tactile graphics. The braille version will likely be more than 300 pages, and the cost per page is higher so the transcribing cost is now more than $1,500. Production cost for the book in three volumes is another $150.

If only modern textbooks were limited to 100 print pages! Most new print textbooks contain more than 500 pages, and 1,500 pages is not unlikely.

Transcribers strive to prepare the textbook in a timely manner so a student has the book as soon as possible, but they also strive to provide a quality product free of errors. They try to accommodate the needs of teachers who skip around, but to make a product that is useful to more than one person, the book must be completed in a systematic way. It takes time. And skill. As Jim Downs noted when he recruited me, men in Georgia's Prison Braille Program had the skills and the time. They knew braille.

Their skills and efforts resulted in a tremendous fiscal benefit for the state, even when one accounted for costs to operate the program. The Department of Corrections incurred costs for a variety of Vocational Education programs whose role was to prepare inmates for life once they were released from prison. Salaries for instructors were part of the annual budget, and it did not matter if the program generated a product used outside of prison. (The Graphic Arts program printed a lot of materials for the Department; students in Heating and Air helped kept ancient systems operating at Scott State Prison; and Masonry or Construction classes provided their services inside the prisons.)

Other costs would be incurred as well: inmates had to be housed and fed whether or not they produced braille; buildings inside the prison had to be maintained whether or not they were used for workspace or storage; the prison had to employ security officers, counselors, food service workers. Inmates cost the state money. Inmates in the Braille Program also saved money for the state. A million dollars over a period of ten years is a conservative estimate of the value of books transcribed and produced in Georgia's prison braille program.

Inmates in the Braille Program cost little more than those in the general population, and they helped defray their fiscal impact on the state by saving money for the Department of Education. In return for the good work they did, we rewarded men who made the long-term commitment to work in the Braille Program with our loyalty.

CHAPTER ELEVEN

Loyalty is nice, but it does little to make life better for a man in prison. Some states allow their vocational programs to pay a small salary to inmates or document their work hours as a way to reduce their sentence. Neither was an option for Georgia's braille transcribers. Still, the men seemed to enjoy the work and the prestige of being part of the Braille Program, at least enough to make it worth their while. Some may also have found their skills and access to craft materials useful as part of the local prison economy.

With or without funds, inmates often find a way to trade goods or services to acquire items they need or want. For those with money on the books, the commissary - or store - stocked items like soup packets, snacks, stamps, and personal care items approved by prison officials. It was supposed to be the only source for such goods, but an inmate might set up shop to shine shoes in exchange for a certain number of stamps. He then might trade the stamps with another inmate to get store goods or even contraband such as tobacco, drugs, alcohol, or time on a cell phone. An inmate might use his knowledge and library time to prepare a letter to a fellow inmate's attorney in order to earn extra food in the chow hall.

There is evidence such bartering has occurred in prisons for centuries. Civil War historian John K. Derden described the prison economy system from Camp Lawton, a short-lived POW camp near Millen, Georgia. The camp was built to relieve crowding at Andersonville, and Derden shared how POWs traded trinkets in their possession - firewood, bricks, blankets - to secure extra food in a camp desperate to meet the needs of its inmates. He described how the inmates hid their belongings so others would not steal them, and how the dire circumstances of winter led some of the Union POWs to take clothing or blankets from the recent dead.

Comparing modern incarceration to a Civil War prison may seem harsh, but it remains true that a prison economy system such as the one Derden described still exists. The system is an important factor in how inmates survive and how administrators manage a prison. Men in prison will do what they can to acquire and hold onto personal items and extra food.

Braille Program inmates often cautioned me to be extra vigilant when inmates from the maintenance crew or another detail worked in our area. They noted the men who were painting or doing electrical work were criminals who would steal anything of value. And, in prison, anything that can be traded is valuable - pens, highlighters, staples, paper.

But as Derden observed in his work on Camp Lawton, the reason for the prison economy system is not limited to personal gain. Then and now, it is often a matter of survival and like the POWs who took care of friends when times got especially difficult, today's inmates do the same.

Inmates may be adequately fed because prisons must follow certain dietary guidelines, but like most of us, inmates sometimes crave more or different foods in their diet. I saw men in the Braille Program share what they had with others. Sometimes they bartered, but often they shared simply because they cared. Bill and I witnessed the caring side of inmates every day, but one Box Day offered a special glimpse of their kindness to one another.

During the holidays, prisons allow inmates to receive a special package of goods from family or friends. This "Box Day" is a special treat, a day when almost everyone gets something from home. The boxes may contain a few costly goodies or a lot, depending on the financial situation of the sender, but the box is a treasure because it is also a message that someone on the outside cares about the inmate.

I recall one holiday Box Day that *Ethan Myers* was visibly upset when he returned from stowing his package. Bill thought he might have been mugged or perhaps received less than expected, but Ethan finally explained his mood. He had realized one of his co-workers was not called out to receive a box at all and thought how unfortunate it was that while most inmates received a bounty of love from home, a few got nothing at all.

The incident reminded me of a conversation I had soon after I started working in prison. I had read an article in a Corrections Association journal in which the author described the concept of inside vs. outside personalities. The article suggested inmates behave in a manner that ensures their survival inside prison; they have very egocentric personalities and rarely give thought to how their actions affect other people. The author went on to suggest it was only after an inmate began to consider others and alter actions accordingly that he or she was ready to be successful with life outside of prison. The words seemed to make sense, at least until I discussed the idea with one of our inmates.

Bud Harper listened politely as I referred to the article and pondered whether one benefit of the Braille Program might be the way it focused attention on the needs of others.

"After all," I said, "it's impossible to transcribe braille without thinking about the reader."

"Bull!" he replied. "There's no such thing as inside vs. outside personality. We're the same people no matter which side of the fence we're on."

An ability to care and consider others was not affected by being in prison - at least according to Bud.

I appreciated his honest response and came to understand Bud's position, even as I clung to the belief that helping someone else by transcribing braille was, indeed, an important milestone for inmates. I saw, as Bud explained, inmates can and do care how their actions impact others, especially the people they love. And, based on my observations, I realized he had a point.

CHAPTER TWELVE

The prison economy and bartering among inmates was no secret to officers. I think some chose to ignore the practice as long as it did not involve serious contraband because the men and women in blue had their hands full with all the other challenges of supervising a thousand or more inmates.

Corrections officers have a difficult job. (Before I started work in the prison a friend stressed that security professionals preferred to be called officers and resent being called "guards.") These professionals in blue monitor everything going on around them and determine how to react to a variety of situations. They write reports, escort non-security personnel like me, assist program managers with inmate traffic in their areas or with their census counts and inmate callouts. An officer must control a room of seventy or more individuals, many of whom reject any and all authority figures and could care less about security protocols. Or, the officer must monitor a large group of men on the yard, an area vulnerable to outsiders tossing contraband over the fence. Security personnel must watch for deals for contraband or situations where opposing groups of inmates might face off with one another.

Corrections officers do these tasks with only a radio and backup from another officer watching from a secure location. The work can be monotonous, tedious, and dangerous. But the men and women who become corrections officers are the first line of defense in maintaining an orderly prison. When disruptions occur, a team of special officers enter the scene.

In their distinctive black uniforms and caps, officers from the CERT team (Corrections Emergency Response Team) make a statement with their presence - and weapons. In addition to the dangerous task of subduing unruly inmates or diffusing situations, CERT team officers conduct inspections, help monitor inmate movement, and escort visiting dignitaries. I observed them to be an elite team of professionals, and like many others in the prison system, the CERT team was ready, willing, and able to protect and serve the public.

There were officers, though, who were less professional. A few - officers who were, perhaps, burned out or anxious to prove themselves - shouted obscenities at inmates or used their voice as a show of force. In my first months at Scott State Prison, I found one officer particularly unprofessional in her treatment of inmates and fellow staff and made up my mind she would serve as a benchmark for me - if I ever became casual about foul language, treated others with such little respect, or began to expect the same behavior from all officers, I would know it was time to end my career in prison.

I realize shouting was necessary sometimes. Prepare for inspection! Chow call! Yard call! Sometimes it was the only way an officer could be heard over the din in tight quarters. I even tried to use my "teacher voice" on a few occasions, but found it less than effective. It was much better for me that when my voice did not rise above the noise, one of the transcribers would whistle loudly to alert everyone to my pending announcement.

I tried to tune out much of the shouting from officers but learned to use it as a signal as well. If certain officers raised their voice or if I heard multiple officers shouting nearby, I recognized it as a signal to stay well out of harm's way. It meant the officers were handling a potentially dangerous situation and did not need to worry about my safety as they did so.

Most officers I knew treated inmates with a certain level of respect, even as they demanded obedience. When I encountered those who were less professional - such as the benchmark officer with the foul mouth or the man in blue berating a young inmate to the point of tears - I tried to consider they were simply troubled souls in the wrong line of work. I reminded myself to think about the officer escorting me to J-Unit who greeted each inmate along the way, calling many of them by name. Or, I would think about men and women like Officer Foston, Officer Bolston, Sergeant Greene, and so many other security personnel who maintained a friendly personality and treated inmates as individuals.

I realize I saw security personnel through a different lens than men in the Braille Program did. Inmates had to submit to orders from officers, but the men in our program also recognized when officers were "just doing their job." They even expressed appreciation for the men and women in blue who treated them fairly.

Perhaps one of the most powerful messages I learned in prison came from observing inmates reciprocate the respect they received from professional corrections officers.

CHAPTER THIRTEEN

The very purpose of correctional facilities demands they function as institutions with staff exercising control over inmates. The institution must ensure the safety of the general public, prison employees, and inmates as well, even as some inmates try to continue behaving as they did outside the fence. Some hold contempt for anyone suggesting they follow a standard of behavior, and others misbehave as a way to survive in the only way they know. Incarcerated individuals have certain rights, but they have little control over much that happens to them inside prison. Multiple daily counts. Crowded living quarters and daily inspections. Random drug testing. Lock downs. Yard call. Store call. Mail call. Chow call. Pill call. Prison routines dictate how inmates live their lives and such routines are characteristic of institutions. Becoming institutionalized is more real for many inmates than the important concept of taking ownership of one's life.

Prison routines had an impact on my life as well, at least for the nine hours I was at work three days a week. Daily counts take precedence over any other activity within the prison. No inmate movement from one location to another is allowed during count, and I came to look forward to the noon count because it offered a bit of quiet on our hall. Count time offered my only opportunity to venture out of J-Unit to trek up the hill alone, but usually I stayed put until my departure at 3:45. When men in the Braille Program went to lunch, I retrieved a small plastic bottle of Dr. Pepper I had left to be refrigerated in the control booth. (Canned drinks were not permitted, even for staff, because prison officials once discovered contraband in soft drink cans.) I could have used the microwave in the control booth to heat something for lunch but usually opted for trail mix instead. I chose that for lunch, in part, because I wanted to avoid eating food the inmates might want. It just didn't feel right to enjoy pizza or tasty meals from home when I knew their menu was limited to institution food. At one point, I adjusted my trail mix recipe after an inmate commented on the yummy-looking M&Ms. He explained they could no longer get the colorful candies in prison because some inmates had used the shells to mix up paints for makeup or temporary tattoos.

Perhaps I did not need to be so sensitive about lunch, but it was clear that bland food and limited access to special treats was a big part of the prison experience. Institutional meals - breakfast, lunch, and supper - prepared on a budget to feed 1,000 men a day. It's no wonder the men asked for pizza and savored days when the aroma of fried chicken signaled they were having "meat with a bone!" Watermelons for the Fourth of July and special treats offered during faith-based events offered some respite from the bland meals, though it did not replace them.

On a few occasions, Bill and I made arrangements for a pizza party donated to express appreciation to the Braille Program for the work they did. A nearby pizza parlor delivered 15-20 large pizzas with cheese, pepperoni, or all the fixings. Every single slice disappeared! That's almost an entire large pizza for every one of the twenty-four inmates in the program. We realized, though, not every slice went to men in our group; they asked to give some to the orderly on our hall, to an aide working nearby, or to the barber next door. The gesture seemed to be their effort to extend goodwill for the program, but it could also have been simply because they cared about others.

One institutional issue with mealtime was the schedule. Inmates took their meals when they were called for chow, and men in the Braille Program often ate breakfast before 7:00 am so they could be ready to start their work day when Bill or I arrived around 7:30. The unit sergeant usually received word for chow call by 11:30 for the men to take their lunch break, but sometimes it did not come until after count cleared. When that happened, the men ate lunch at 12:30 or 1:30. The delay was not unbearable, but the Braille Unit dorm was usually called to dinner as early as 4:30. Inmates spent their long evenings between meals sorting through store goods for a snack to tide them over until morning.

Sometimes, inmates pooled their resources to share, and birthdays or other occasions offered a celebration with the dorm's most creative cook preparing a special meal from their stash. I remember once at Scott when I questioned why the supply of new, clear trash bags was diminishing so rapidly, Bud explained they were preparing for Ethan's birthday. He said their "chain gang chef" would combine various ingredients, pour them into the bag, and cook over the radiator in the dorm. (I'm not sure how they would have managed had the celebration been in July.) I witnessed the creativity of the Braille Program's chef during our professional development workshop. He cut trash bags into squares to wrap a tortilla filled with tuna and other ingredients from their store supplies. It looked tasty and the men offered to share the treat, but I am not a fan of tuna.

I suppose, then, some inmates understood all that is involved with planning and preparing meals - budgeting resources, time, etc.. Most, though, expected their meals to be served without question and voiced only their dissatisfaction with the quality. It was, after all, institution food. Though the men in the Braille Program filled their days with work, I often thought about how my day was not done when I drove away from the prison at 4:00. I still had to shop for groceries, prepare a meal, do laundry. They didn't. Living the institutional life meant clothing and food issued by someone else. It also meant chores done by designated inmate details because the prison had to control access to the kitchen, laundry, or other areas vulnerable to contraband, escape attempts, or criminal behaviors.

There were other factors of prison life that highlighted its institutional nature. Daily activities were planned and dictated by others. The prison controlled who entered its gates so inmates saw only those people administrators and security saw fit to allow inside. Inmates wore white uniforms issued and laundered by the prison, along with bright yellow slickers for rainy days or light blue jackets to break the chill of a cold wind. When an item of clothing wore out or needed repair, an inmate notified personnel so he could exchange it for a replacement. Shoes, most of them black leather, provided an opportunity for some men to show pride in their appearance; they polished the toes to a high gloss. And, if approved to wear soft shoes, they kept their tennis shoes clean and bright white. When we moved to Central, some men were frustrated they could no longer meticulously iron their uniforms, but they found a way to press a nice sharp crease in their pants even without a steam iron. The crisp appearance of some men contrasted with others who seemed satisfied to wear dingy uniforms until the warden or another member of the inspection team demanded he do better. At least when we had Open House or other important visitors, almost all the men in the Braille Program made the effort to look their best.

Even when I considered the differences in our after-work responsibilities, I realized I had the freedom to leave the confines of prison each day. I could choose how to balance chores with recreation. I did not have an authority figure dictating how I spent my time away from work. Inmates might visit with friends as they walked through the compound or exercised on the yard. They could attend faith-based events in the evening or read books they checked out of the prison library. But, inmates had to adhere to the strict count protocol, and security personnel could hold them in the dorm if necessary or deny their request to go to the library.

The inmates had little control over when and where they spent their time after work. As one inmate told me, he and others knew precisely when they could do what they wanted: "on Wednesday - whens dey let us do it." I appreciated the sense of humor some maintained about the concept of being institutionalized.

The prison library offered an escape from the drudgery of long evenings in the dorm so it was a very popular call-out for inmates. Many also used reference materials in the library to research legal matters related to their case (or, for a fellow inmate). Much like chow call, yard call, or store call, inmates were permitted to visit the library only at their scheduled time, and our isolation in the J-Unit often put our group out-of-sight and out-of-mind for the library staff. To ensure the men didn't miss the coveted privilege, Bill or I would often call the library early in the day their dorm was scheduled to go to the library to ask if men in the Braille Program were on the list, but mostly to jog their memory. The transcribers took the initiative to ask the librarian to schedule their call-out late in the day so it did not disrupt their work day too much and so they would not have an extra trip to make across the compound.

Books, food, recreation, mail call. Those were welcome breaks from the routine of an inmate's institutional life. None of those compared, though, to visitation. I never witnessed the important weekend process, but knowing the protocol for visitors coming in to the Braille Program and hearing the men talk about visitation, I have an idea of the scene. Visitors - family or friends with prior approval from the prison - filled the parking lot on Saturday or Sunday or a holiday. After driving from distances far and near, they waited in line, sometimes for hours in the sun or cold or rain. Four people at a time would be allowed into the sally port of the "shake-down" shack to sign in, submit their ID, proceed through a metal detector, and potentially be scanned with an electronic wand to ensure they were not carrying contraband. Then the visitors proceeded through another security point before being allowed into the large open room to spend an hour with the inmate. Though the short visit took place in a crowded noisy room monitored by officers, inmates considered it time well spent. I avoided discussing personal matters with inmates, but they often shared news from home or showed off new photos after their visitation weekends.

For inmates whose families lived too far away or lacked the financial means to visit the prison, or the men whose families had given up and chose not to visit, weekends were simply two more long days inside the fence. All of the men spent their lives inside an institution, and some were better prepared to transition to a life outside.

CHAPTER FOURTEEN

Inmates look forward to the day they might transfer out of prison to a transition center or to the freedom they earned after serving their entire sentence. They generally do not, however, look forward to being transferred to another prison.

Protocol for prison transfers involves inspections, shackles, and more inspections, including personal inspection as warranted. The process is not pleasant, and when I realized it was protocol even for the daily trip between Men's and Scott State Prisons, I had even greater appreciation for the eleven inmates who endured the same ordeal four days each week in order to be part of our consolidated Braille Program.

When Scott State Prison closed in 2009, men in the Braille Program submitted to the transfer process as did all inmates from the facility. The transcribers were fortunate that most were transferred directly to Central, but that does not mean they took a direct route between Milledgeville and Macon. I was familiar with the roads between the two cities, and except for the short daylight driving hours of winter, I had come to enjoy the commute each morning and afternoon. I knew where to be especially vigilant for deer crossing the highway, where to expect more or less traffic, and I knew I would arrive at my destination within about 40 minutes. It took the men in the Braille Program much longer.

First, inmates had to be processed through the Georgia Diagnostic and Classification State Prison in Jackson, a jaunt that added more than eighty miles to the trip. They went through inspection early in the morning, were shackled, and then boarded a bus in Milledgeville. The inmates carried their belongings with them and shuffled through inspection when they arrived in Jackson. Then, late in the day, the men arrived in Macon where they went through still another inspection before being assigned a bed at Central State Prison. The journey took them an entire day.

A day spent in shackles, interacting with various security personnel. A day which offered a glimpse of the outside world through the wire mesh windows of a bus. At least Braille Program inmates traveled together as a group and avoided the stress of being alone to adapt to a new place and a new population of inmates.

None of us involved with the Braille Program had control over that or any transfer, though Bill had influence with the administrators who supported our plea to keep as many inmates with the program as possible. Prison officials must consider several variables before approving placement of an inmate at a particular prison: the security level of the prison (close, medium, or minimum); the inmate's criminal background; level of medical care provided in the facility and whether the inmate has significant medical issues; programs within the prison and whether the inmate requires specific courses to prepare him for release; politics; proximity to family and/or victims.

The transfers that resulted from the closure of Scott State Prison may have been beyond the norm for any of us in the Braille Program, but we had experienced a variety of individual transfers through the years. When possible, Bill and I tried to determine why the transfer took place and if we had the option to rescind the transfer of a valuable member of our team. Sometimes, if it was the result of a clerical error, the individual might return within a week or two after we brought the issue to the Deputy Warden's attention. Other times, though, if the warden made it clear we could not intervene we understood it was time to close the conversation.

Beyond asking where an inmate was sent, Bill and I never tried to intervene if we knew the transfer was a positive move for the individual. In fact, whenever a man was sent to the Transition Center, Bill worked closely with staff in the new facility to explain our program and help their staff find a way to accommodate the inmate's effort to continue working with braille while he proceeded toward release from prison.

Medical transfers often presented a dilemma for inmates in the Braille Program. If his medical needs exceeded the general dental and health care provided at Central, the inmate faced a temporary transfer to Augusta State Medical Prison (ASMP). Men in our program tried to avoid the transfers unless the need was significant because they did not want the hassle involved - security protocols (personal inspection and shackles), an all-day bus ride across the state, temporary assignment to ASMP and losing their current bed assignment at Central, being gone for at least two nights but likely a week or more. Transfers took place on Tuesday or Thursday, and the men often did not know about their transfer until late at night when an officer ordered them to pack their stuff and report for inspection.

Whenever possible, the men sent word to Bill and me. Prison administrators did not have the luxury of being able to hold vacant beds, but the men knew we would do what we could to keep their spot in the Braille Program open so when they returned to Central they could return to their studies and work assignments as soon as possible.

Whatever the reason for a transfer, if the men knew what was happening, they tried to send word about the status of their current work. They wanted to ensure braille volumes continued to go out for students, even if it meant assigning the work to a fellow inmate. It was one more example of the professionalism I saw develop as inmates became transcribers.

CHAPTER FIFTEEN

A quote attributed to Henry Ford suggests:

"Business needs more of the professional spirit. The professional spirit seeks professional integrity from pride, not from compulsion. The professional spirit detects its own violations and penalizes them."

Braille transcribers - the volunteers who learn to braille in their spare time so they can help individuals who are blind as well as the people who strive to make a living by providing the valuable service - demonstrate Ford's professional spirit. They take pride in doing the highest quality work because they want braille readers to have the best product possible.

Like most other transcribers in prison braille programs I met through the years, men in our program knew we expected a lot from them, that we expected them to take pride in a job well done. They understood that meeting our expectations offered an opportunity to prove to the world they were capable of doing good things.

As Ford suggested, the professional spirit includes detecting its own violations, and inmates in the Braille Program learned to do just that, particularly when it came to making decisions about the material they were transcribing. Sometimes, it was a fellow inmate who detected a violation of the braille rules, and even when it resulted in an intense discussion among team members, the lead transcriber learned to handle the criticism, to own his work - good or bad. Like so many other inmates trying to move toward life on the outside, men in our program had little tolerance for their peers who did not own their mistakes. If the discussion resulted in a need to correct the braille, the transcriber did so and moved on to the next challenge. Perhaps the attitude about owning their mistakes in braille helped reinforce the concept in other parts of their lives as well.

We may have seen demonstrations of the professional integrity Ford promoted, but Bill and I also recognized an institutional mindset about personal property. We expected the men to demonstrate prudent use of supplies in the program and not stash them away for personal use, but we knew it happened. Some men considered a supply of glue or string in their desk as their personal property, even if it came from the supplies we provided. We monitored such items and expected the men to let us know if a ream of paper ran out or an ink cartridge ran dry. We readily supplied more, sometimes noting if we thought excessive amounts were being used. Because they knew I was personally responsible for some materials like thread or beads, many transcribers limited their personal use, except during holidays when they wanted to create a special card to send a loved one.

Bill and I monitored the supplies as a matter of fiscal responsibility, to try to teach the men a small business skill. They had to learn to manage inventory, including supplies. But, we also wanted to make sure the Braille Program was not implicated in supplying contraband such as ink, markers, and other materials. Another reason to monitor the ink and glue cartridges used in the program was that, in the wrong hands, the hard plastic or metal parts could pose a safety hazard or the ink could be used by chain gang tattoo artists. I took the cartridges out with me, recycling the ink at a local office supply store where I could use the credit to purchase poster boards or other materials we used for tactile graphics.

In addition to fiscal responsibility, we tried to promote workplace safety as part of our professional spirit. The concept was important in a prison where sharp instruments could become weapons in the wrong hands.

For instance, each morning I exchanged brass chits engraved with my name with an officer who checked out a box of spur wheels, small scissors, and assorted other tools to me. The set included a very large pair of scissors attached to a cable with a padlock; I secured the scissors to a table in the work room. We counted tools in the morning, at lunch time, and then collected them before inmates left in the afternoon. At Scott State Prison, Officer Foston delivered and retrieved the tools from a secure location on our floor. He and I signed a paper at the end of the day when I returned all the tools and he returned the chit to me. When the program moved to Central State Prison, Bill and I checked out tools in the administration building and walked through the compound. After a year of that practice, the warden approved a plan to secure the tools in a locked area within our locked office. Each afternoon, I had to collect all the tools and confirm with the unit's sergeant or another officer all the tools were present before I could leave the prison.

In addition to the tool box, we accounted for the small dull stylus men used to manually punch in braille cells and for computer flash drives the men used to store files and share with one another.

I'm sure men in the Braille Program could have (perhaps, would have) used the tools and materials for inappropriate purposes. After all, they lived and had to survive in prison, and they were very creative. But, I never worried about the men having access to scissors and sharp tools. They were essential for an important transcribing task the men needed to learn. Most of the transcribers maintained a kit of glue, strings, and other bits of material, and they used the tools to create tactile graphics - raised interpretations of textbook

The small, blunt-tip scissors in our tool kit were made for young children. They did not fit well in the hands of large men and were notoriously fragile, so the men became expert at rigging up a repair. I was impressed and finally commented on the their ability to produce fine tactile graphics with our less-than-perfect tools. One of the transcribers showing me the intricate pieces of a raised map explained he was not using the scissors; he was using a razor blade from his kit. Razor blade!

Ricky Camden showed me the kit he kept in his drawer. It contained the blade from a disposable razor, wrapped with tape on one side so he could use it without cutting his hand as he cut out small curved shapes in thick chipboard. He had a small bottle of glue and lengths of his favorite thread to ensure he had a consistent supply for all the tactile graphics in his current textbook project. Ricky didn't need to explain the nail clippers in his kit; I had already learned to use a pair to cut plastic straps off cases of paper since I, too, did not have ready access to a decent pair of scissors. As the inmate shared his personal tool kit with me I realized I was not the only person contributing to the needs of the program. I never asked how/when the men brought razor blades into the program area, and we never had Security write up an inmate for such items, even if they might have confiscated them during inspection. The men took pride in their creativity, and their problem-solving served our program well.

Another workplace skill Bill and I sought to instill was professional courtesy. Perhaps because of my Southern background or because of the generation in which I grew up, I consider the manner in which we refer to colleagues as important. For instance, I always referred to my boss at the Academy for the Blind as Dr. Hyer and would never think to use his first name. Though I knew the President of the American Printing House for the Blind as a friend and called him Tuck at times, I always used the more formal Dr. Tinsley when greeting him or referring to him in professional contexts. In much the same way, I made it clear from the first day on the job the men should refer to me as Mrs. Amerson. In return, I added "Mr." when I called their names, something most prison staff would not do. Because of our effort, I was peeved when one ex-offender sent word in a card to "Say hi to Bill and Marie." It seemed his way of saying, "I'm out of prison and no longer have to follow your rules," a sentiment Dr. Hyer confirmed he had experienced with former students he saw after they graduated from the Academy. For the most part, though, men in the Braille Program understood my preference for using formal names in the workplace. Like me, some even maintained the professional courtesy after they moved to the other side of the fence as well. I admit, though, I was touched by one effort to alter the practice.

I learned early on that the men often used nicknames, or street names, for one another. It was their way of showing affection. Though I continued to use the more formal Mr. Myers or Mr. Deaton, it surprised some of the men when they realized I actually knew their casual monikers too - Chip, Jersey, Chen, and Gramps. One day several months after I started, Roger Deaton proposed a nickname for me.

"Mrs. Amerson, would you mind if we call you Ma - you know, since your initials are M.A. and you're kinda like a mom?"

I was amused. I was honored. But I was not convinced accepting the change in our protocol would be a good idea. They may have referred to me as Ma in the dorm or when I was not around, but the men continued to offer me the courtesy of using my formal name.

It was one more example of their professionalism and I think Mr. Henry Ford would be impressed by the spirit of men in Georgia's Braille Program. They worked with pride in their product and in themselves, they strove to follow protocol and maintain a good reputation, and they searched for ways to improve our program.

CHAPTER SIXTEEN

When I joined the Braille Program at Scott State Prison, I did so to help the program improve and grow. I knew I didn't know a lot about braille and even less about working with inmates, but thankfully, I had a wealth of mentors. In the prison, vocational education staff like Mr. Grimes, Mr. Snow, and Ms. Johnson helped guide me through the daily chores and reports required of a civilian employee. Officer Foston and other staff helped steady my balance between being a trusting educator who had worked with young students with visual impairments and being someone who taught adults with varying motives for their actions.

Bill Hinton was one of my strongest mentors in the prison. When we met in 2006, Bill was Senior Manager for the Programs Division for Georgia Department of Corrections. His role involved supervising Education Services and Workforce Development for Georgia's prisons, and in that capacity, Bill had met with Jim Downs to discuss an inter-agency agreement for operating the Braille Program. When Bill retired from the Department of Corrections in 2008, his successor convinced him to contract as a general program consultant. His new role included overseeing the consolidation of the two Braille Programs in Milledgeville, and eventually, Bill eased into a part-time position to help ensure the program operated four days a week. Though our schedules rarely overlapped to allow us both to be in prison on the same day, Bill and I maintained an open line of communication. We left notes for one another and talked on the phone. Each of us knew issues the other faced, and if inmates asked one of us for approval to do something, we had our partner's position on the issue before we gave a response - just in case the men tried to get Ma and Pa to give different answers.

With his increased exposure to the Braille Program and inmates who had taken on the new profession, Bill became convinced it was like no other program in the prison system. As a former warden and district administrator, he added a tremendous presence to the program, and his networking expertise proved especially valuable for inmates preparing to transition out of prison.

Before he dedicated all his work hours to the Braille Program, Bill was an enthusiastic guest at our first Open House. Later, he became an even more enthusiastic host. The event took on greater importance as Bill expanded the invitation list to include officials from the Pardons and Parole Board and other administrators he had worked with in the field of Corrections. We hosted visits from such officials throughout the year, and Bill always made a priority of noting particular inmates who were demonstrating an important goal of the prison system - they were men working toward being successful outside of prison so they would never return. We offered anecdotal data from the National Prison Braille Network which indicated the recidivism rate for ex-offenders from such programs was close to zero. I have no doubt that Bill's well-respected opinion led to a positive comment or two as inmates came up for parole consideration. For that, I am forever thankful.

Before Bill joined the Braille Program in 2008, I had felt lost in my efforts to help inmates transition to a successful career in transcribing. I knew people in the field of blindness. I knew ex-offenders *could* be successful as braille transcribers and find work. I knew that, as contractors, men could work from their homes for agencies all across the nation. What I did not know was how to help them secure equipment, supplies, and materials, or how to avail themselves of general support services for ex-offenders. Together, Bill and I improved our program's transition planning for the transcribers. I focused on matters specific to braille while he worked to secure approval for inmates in a Transition Center to have access to a computer with braille translation software and the opportunity to maintain their braille skills while completing other portions of the program. While I networked with the blindness field to locate work opportunities and stay abreast of trends in braille transcription, Bill helped Transition Center staff understand that a contract to transcribe braille was legitimate employment.   We helped men in the program understand that even if they had to secure traditional employment, they could also complete braille contracts and develop a good reputation with agencies seeking quality braille textbooks.

Bill's contribution to the success of the Braille Program and its graduates was critical. So, too, was the support of Jim Downs who encouraged ex-offenders to contact his office so they could seek contracts to transcribe books for the Georgia Instructional Materials Center. Jim allowed us to lend braille translation software to the men as they transitioned out of prison, and he offered suggestions for how/where individuals might purchase or lease computer equipment. Other staff in Jim's office also helped, such as when a business owner contacted GIMC. He wanted to know if a particular ex-offender was serious about his work as a transcriber and whether he would make good use of the equipment he was buying. The GIMC staff member contacted me to confirm their answer and the transcriber who was just starting out on his own was able to purchase a critical piece of equipment at a deep discount.

Support from prison officials and co-workers, from the Department of Education, and from agencies and business owners in the field of blindness allowed the Braille Program to see great success.

CHAPTER SEVENTEEN

Success can be defined in several ways. For me, one way to do so was the ever-improving ability of our program to deliver quality products for Georgia's students who read braille. I also defined success with the way former participants talked about their experiences in the program and how those impacted their lives. Parole. Reduced recidivism. Working as an independent braille transcriber. Living positively and contributing to their family and community outside the fence. Finding their own definitions of success as an ex-offender.

Getting out of prison is one thing; staying out is another matter, and Corrections officials consider low recidivism as a marker of success. Recidivism is a term related to convicted criminals who re-offend, especially repeatedly, and find themselves back in prison. Parole boards have the unenviable task of considering recidivism and determining whether an inmate is likely to stay out of trouble once he or she is released from prison. They must use their best judgement to determine if an individual has skills for potential employment, if the inmate has a support system of family or friends, whether the individual has a plan for success once he or she is out. Members of the parole board need to know they can expect the ex-offender will avoid negative influences so he or she will stay out of prison.

Prisons help inmates spend their time inside preparing to get out. The institutions provide classes to help inmates acquire a general education diploma (GED) or learn vocational trades. Counselors operate programs to address substance abuse. But even as the corrections system tries to find ways to help inmates succeed when they leave prison, they treat everyone as a criminal, someone who cannot be trusted to do the right thing. For their part, inmates walk the fine line of balancing a need to demonstrate they are not like their peers with the need to fit in, to behave in ways that keep them safe and sane inside the fence.

Sometimes inmates find the best way to change their lives is to seek positive experiences inside prison. Many attend faith-based activities or take every opportunity to learn something new. Georgia's Braille Program certainly offered the challenge of new learning, and though not based on religion, the experience of creating a product for someone else offered a real-time demonstration of empathy and caring. Participants came to hope their work might garner the positive attention of the parole board, that it would help them secure release. And though our aim was to prepare the men for success as independent braille transcribers, Bill and I often reminded inmates to also consider additional career options as well.

As difficult as it is to admit, I did not expect every man who came through the program to become a successful braille transcriber when he left prison. Some transcribers were good enough when they were part of a team who could catch errors or help ensure a correctly formatted textbook. Others needed the structure of our long work days where everyone was expected to be on task with braille throughout the day; without it they would likely become distracted by a multitude of other tasks. Some individuals did not demonstrate potential for managing a small business which, because of the nature of independent contracts, most needed to know. Even though business training was not one of my strengths, I tried to provide access to resources and references to help explain small business concepts. Thankfully, several men had learned the concepts in other vocational training activities or through self-study, and they were willing to share their knowledge with teammates.

I learned the importance of business training from discussions with the National Prison Braille Network, a group that met each year in conjunction with the Annual Meeting of the American Printing House for the Blind (APH). Members of the network included braille program administrators with backgrounds in corrections work along with educators and former inmates. The group offered insight on the skills and supports that would provide better opportunities for transcribers leaving prison, including the skills associated with being an independent contractor.

This network of professionals also taught me that agencies around the United States expected high-quality braille from former inmates because the men and women learned in prison as part of a team. The network noted a willingness from braille service providers to give ex-offenders a chance; the agencies relied on the reputation of the program in which an inmate learned to transcribe braille, but more importantly, they relied on the individual's work as a recommendation for subsequent contracts. Ex-offenders could prove themselves worthy of continued opportunities.

Bill and I used advice from the National Prison Braille Network to prepare a transition packet. We understood it would be especially difficult for some to take the initiative to contact a stranger about work, so we provided contact information for APH, the Georgia Instructional Materials Center, and other important potential employers in the field of blindness. We tried to provide appropriate reference materials and braille translation software, and we tried to find ways to help men secure equipment. Even as we prepared information and provided support, we expected ex-offenders to take steps on their own, too, not an easy thing for someone who has been told what to do and when for so many years.

Transition Centers offer one avenue for moving out of prison and into the success we sought for program participants. Such centers provide support and challenge inmates to find employment even as they help them locate potential jobs, understand how to complete applications, and prepare to handle a discussion about their criminal history. The ex-offender must still report for daily counts, but a Transition Center offers a less structured setting so an individual can learn to budget his time. He also learns to budget finances so there is money available to pay rent or buy groceries and gas. The supportive staff in a Transition Center helps an ex-offender ease back into the community.

Most inmates seek any opportunity to earn their freedom, whether through a Transition Center, being released on parole, or reaching their "max-out" date. I am haunted, though, by one or two men for whom such freedom might not have been their goal, men who were most at home among fellow inmates.

Arthur Smith was one such individual. His friends in the Braille Program lobbied for the timid inmate to pass his remaining time in prison with us, assuring Bill and me he would not cause any problems. Since he would not have time to really learn braille textbook transcribing, we agreed to let Arthur join us to help with digital textbook conversions.

Arthur had been in prison more than ten years so he knew how to follow rules. He came to work and kept to himself most of the time. Occasionally, Arthur would assure me he was doing his best to learn his job, and he always expressed appreciation for being part of the program. As his max-out date neared, I saw Arthur's anxiety rise. He shared with me that his only close relative - his mother - had died while he was serving his time and he was not sure where he would live when he left prison. He did not know anyone on the outside and confessed his only friends were men he would leave behind. Arthur knew he had to find work, but he did not know what kind of employment he would be able to secure. His anxiety suggested to me that Arthur felt comfortable and was most "at home" in prison so I felt bad seeing him worry about his future.

There were others, too, who may have struggled to move into a new life when they left prison. *Fred* and *Dennis* went to a nursing home when they left prison, trading one institution for another. Another may have returned to his roots on the street, wheeling and dealing to survive, and since his braille skills were marginal at best, I often thought *Walter* might become the negative statistic from our program by returning to prison.

I hope I am wrong about the bleak future of some ex-offenders from our program, and I take comfort in knowing several Braille Program graduates who did find success outside the fence.

Paul Young works a regular forty-hour-a-week job and does contract braille work for a group in his community. Ricky Camden, who always expressed doubt he could succeed as a transcriber, works at a machine shop in his home state; he makes a living for his family and strives to never return to prison. *Alton Morris* uses computer skills he honed in the program in his work at a metro-Atlanta facility that helps ex-offenders find work and adjust to life outside of prison.

These men are using skills they learned inside - along with faith and a resolve to do better. They are honoring their families and loved ones by staying out of trouble. They are becoming a positive force in their communities. And all of these ex-offenders set examples for other men in the Braille Program, whether they transcribe braille for a living or simply hold that experience as part of their past.

Of course, I was pleased to have a leading example of success in the field of braille transcription, and it happened to also be an individual who highlighted an idea we often promoted - ex-offenders should consider alternative/additional employment as they strive to become braille transcribers on the outside.

I had watched *Cam Johnson* grow in his confidence about his braille skills and saw his diligence as a student in the Braille Program. He seemed very motivated to succeed when he left prison and had excellent family support. Upon his release, Cam contacted the Georgia Instructional Materials Center to secure contract work, but he also operated a lawn-care service in his community. Cam cut grass during the day then transcribed braille textbooks at night. He located and bought a used thermoform machine to use for tactile graphics, and very quickly, the ex-offender established a reputation as an excellent, dependable braille transcriber.

Cam relayed a message to his former colleagues - succeeding on the outside was not easy, but it could happen. Several months after his release from prison, Cam shared news in another message. He had been hired by a program that provided accessible materials to college students. We all celebrated the news and his former co-workers saw how Cam's hard work paid off. In spite of a criminal record, he held a salaried position in an agency where he had the respect of professional colleagues. Several months later, the agency hired a second graduate of Georgia's Braille Program, and I was quite proud of the two men who displayed so much professionalism in their work.

Even as I took pride in their employment success, I also appreciated how Cam's eventual departure from the position also offered an important lesson for men in the Braille Program.

Cam had accepted the prestigious salaried position in order to support the family who stood with him during and after his incarceration. He made a commitment to the job even though the long daily commute added four hours to his eight-hour work day. Eventually, the long days at work and away from his family took its toll. Cam had witnessed the fall of a fellow ex-offender whose work had opened many doors in the field. She had taken on too many commitments, and Cam saw his friend slip back into a pattern of seeking comfort from alcohol. Rather than put himself under similar stress, Cam resigned the full-time position and returned to transcribing braille as an independent contractor while he also operated a lawn-care service. With fewer hours on the road and away from home, Cam found time to go fishing with his father and spend precious time with his young son.

The decision to step back from a high-profile full-time job demonstrated a philosophy I had heard Cam explain - it's up to an individual to take ownership of his life, to know he is responsible for his own happiness and troubles. Cam apparently understood taking ownership sometimes meant making difficult decisions and an individual must do what is right for himself and his family.

I believe he demonstrated that, sometimes, success outside the fence is about more than money.

As I began writing this memoir, two more inmates from the Braille Program were making the transition out of prison. Like their predecessors, these men knew it would not be easy to find employment, but Cam and *Gary Thompson* inspired them to hope. The inmates knew they had unique skills, and we had all learned their status as an ex-offender mattered less to braille readers than the quality of their work.

At the 2013 annual workshop for Georgia's Teachers of the Visually Impaired (TVI), Roger Deaton - a graduate of the Braille Program who had been released from prison six months before - teamed up with me to help a local school system TVI discuss quality braille for students. After the presentation, a participant asked Roger if he might travel to her state to help train braille transcribers. He and I were gratified to realize the educator saw Roger's professionalism and skills, not his past mistakes.

Several months later, I received an email from Roger with a simple subject line - "Gratitude." He was writing on his first day of full-time employment with an accessible media agency to say thank you for a letter of support I had sent the agency. I appreciated the gesture and feel sure my letter of support was only a small part of his success.

Roger, Cam, Gary, and others were responsible for their own success. They demonstrated a commitment to braille inside the fence. They learned braille code, textbook formatting, proofreading. They worked to earn certificates in Nemeth code for mathematics and Music braille. As these men left prison and entered the world of work on the outside, they paved the way for each other. They took the initiative to secure supplies, equipment, and assignments. As much as I would like to claim some responsibility for their success, I know it was their hard work that made the biggest difference. Still, I am gratified to know they appreciated my small part in the process.

I know from their feedback, my role with the Braille Program meant something to the men.

Not long after Cam Johnson started his full-time position with the agency that provided accessible media to college students, his employer contacted me with a request. They faced a tight deadline and needed to borrow braille paper. Since the prison was close to Cam's home, they asked if he could stop by and pick up several boxes. They would have the supplier ship replacements directly to us within a week or two. That afternoon I carted two heavy boxes of braille paper out to my car and waited.

What a thrill to see Cam Johnson drive into the parking lot, to see him wearing street clothes and walking outside the razor wire that surrounded my workplace. The young man beamed as he got out of his car and asked if he could give me a hug, something he would never have done as an inmate. He expressed great appreciation for his current employment situation and as we transferred braille paper to his car, Cam noted the irony of this particular errand.

"Mrs. Amerson, you just don't know the chill bumps I got driving in here. It was exactly one year ago today when I walked out of here and said I'd never be back."

I got chill bumps too, right along with a lump in my throat as I watched him drive away again. Thinking I might have been a small part of Cam's success kept me going in the program for another few years.

Cam was also part of another incident that helped me understand the impact a good Braille Program can have on inmates' lives. Gary Thompson, another graduate of our program, joined Cam in the accessible materials center at the college. Both men attended the National Prison Braille Forum in Louisville, Kentucky, and during the meeting, their agency presented information about an innovative Federal project. Both graduates explained how their experience in our Braille Program helped prepare them for current responsibilities with the project, and I couldn't help but smile with pride. Then, during the 2012 forum, Cam and Gary were among friends and colleagues who recognized me for my years of service in the field. Hearing them say I had made a difference in their lives touched my heart.

Author Rick Bragg noted in his book *All Over But the Shoutin'*: "Every life deserves a certain amount of dignity, no matter how poor or damaged the shell that carries it." I believe that is correct, and perhaps the warm hugs and expressions of gratitude from former inmates suggest I succeeded in my efforts to treat men in the Braille Program with dignity and respect.

Such respect - given and received - is my definition of success. It is worth more than gold.

CHAPTER EIGHTEEN

Throughout my career in the blindness field, I knew about the American Printing House for the Blind (APH). It is the oldest company in the U.S. dedicated to creating and distributing educational materials in accessible formats for blind and visually impaired students at the pre-college level. APH - a 501(c)(3) private, nonprofit organization - receives an annual federal appropriation through the U.S. Department of Education. The Printing House employees an in-house team of highly qualified braille transcribers, and they subcontract with about 350 individual transcribers and groups across the country in order to meet the demand for braille textbooks.

As part of my responsibilities at the Georgia Academy for the Blind, each year I attended the APH Annual Meeting in Louisville, Kentucky. Even after I retired from the school, I continued to attend the October event to participate in one of several "related meetings" that took place while so many professional colleagues from the small field were gathered in one location. One such meeting was the American Foundation for the Blind Solutions Forum, a grassroots effort involving educators, publishers, and others interested in improving access to learning materials for students who were print disabled. A particular concern of the Solutions Forum highlighted the need for additional braille transcribers. APH staff responded with a suggestion that prison braille programs around the country might be able to help address that concern.

During the 2001 Solutions Forum, I learned of another related meeting taking place as part of the APH Annual Meeting - the National Prison Braille Forum. Corrections staff, educators, and ex-offenders gathered to share highlights of their programs, discuss challenges in their operations, and collect ideas from one another. APH staff hoped the activity would give greater visibility to prison braille programs and point to one solution for the need for additional braille transcribers.

It was not until I started working in prison in 2006 that I attended my first Prison Braille Forum. As I listened to individuals introduce themselves, it occurred to me that everyone at the table was a professional interested in helping prison braille programs and their graduates succeed. Though I had been working in the prison braille program for six months, I think that was the moment I understood how powerful the programs could be in offering hope and opportunity, and why the field of blindness was a perfect environment for such training. My years in special education had taught me our field held close the concept that an individual's abilities are more important than their disabilities. I saw that perhaps the concept could also relate to focusing on an individual's current abilities and actions instead of their past misdeeds. The forum and the network of prison braille professionals demonstrated to me the benefits for braille readers and ex-offenders alike.

In particular, two individuals I met at my first Prison Braille Forum stand out in memory. Today, in fact, I count both of them among my friends in the field of blindness.

A few months after the October 2006 forum, Nancy Lacewell, APH's Director of Government and Community Affairs, invited several prison braille program administrators, representatives of the National Braille Association, transcriber groups, ex-offenders, and U.S. Department of Justice officials to participate in a focus group. The purpose of the group was to assist APH in preparing information for a possible grant to help ex-offenders transition to work outside of prison. Ex-offenders *Robert Evans* and *Annette Barwick* articulated some of the challenges they faced in learning braille, and more importantly, challenges they faced in finding a way to use their specialized skills to earn a living once they walked out the gates of a prison. In spite of the challenges, both ex-offenders echoed a sentiment I heard many times in the years I worked with inmates - the braille program changed their lives. Annette went so far as to say her success in learning braille and becoming a highly qualified transcriber had saved her life.

Annette had a history of substance abuse and multiple incarcerations. She was languishing in prison when staff at the large correctional facility in Texas allowed her to enter the braille program. As Annette learned braille, she began to see herself as a competent, capable person, one who could succeed in life instead of continuing her existence as an addict with little hope. She used the new-found self-confidence to turn her life around, and as she benefitted from opportunities outside of prison, Annette made a point of trying to help other ex-offenders. She became involved in organizations in the field and offered a strong voice on the professionalism of those transcribers who learned braille in prison.

Robert, too, talked about the changes a braille program brought to his life. He said he realized the powerful impact of being respected by others and saw his self-esteem rise as he took opportunities afforded by his skills as a braille transcriber. He hoped that other ex-offenders could have similar opportunities so they, too, could move forward with productive lives.

Annette and Robert cautioned the focus group - success outside of prison requires a strong support system. Like every other ex-offender, a braille transcriber needs the general support of family and community, but they also need a network of people who understand the specialized work they do. The equipment and software required for transcribing books into braille is not cheap, and since a transcriber can only be paid for work he or she has completed, financial assistance or some type of resource loan is important for the new contractor. It is also important to have actual transcription work because braille is a "use it or lose it" skill which can fade quickly without practice.

The information Annette and Robert shared opened my eyes to the transition issues for braille transcribers, and along with subsequent Prison Braille Forums, helped me see the issues more clearly. In addition to strong braille skills, inmates need small business skills; they need advice and contacts for networking in a field that requires the products they create; inmates need help explaining to parole officials - and even their families - how braille transcription contracts are real work; men and women who have spent five, ten, or more years behind bars need to understand how to budget limited resources and time to ensure they can complete jobs and get paid. I came to understand the men and women who learn braille in prison need all this, and at the same time, they need the skills and stamina to cope with a society that does not always welcome ex-offenders.

Challenges I faced with work seemed small in comparison to those of the ex-offenders I met through the Prison Braille Forum, but my experiences with the group challenged me to find ways to make Georgia's program the best it could be. Each visit to Louisville and the Prison Braille Forum renewed my appreciation for the work we accomplished at Scott and Central State Prisons.

My appreciation for the National Prison Braille Forum continued to grow over the years as I met new program graduates striving to succeed as independent transcribers, form a small business with a group of their peers, or demonstrate their professionalism to an agency willing to take a chance on hiring an ex-offender. I saw friends achieve more such as when Robert took a position directing a prison braille program; Annette served on the board of the National Braille Association; Georgia graduates Cam Johnson and Gary Thompson became an integral part of their agency's curriculum development so other prisons might offer braille training programs. All of the ex-offenders I met through the National Prison Braille Network seemed to appreciate their new careers, and they always seemed to make a point of trying to help others.

Such experiences suggest to me the National Prison Braille Network is an important component in the mission of the American Printing House for the Blind. That mission says APH will promote independence of blind and visually impaired persons by providing specialized materials, products, and services needed for education and life. Whether they are individuals who learned braille in a program inspired by the National Prison Braille Network, men and women who participated in training offered by APH staff visiting a prison, or individuals whose program adapted training to ensure their team produced textbooks to meet APH criteria, the highly qualified transcribers from prison braille programs help APH accomplish their mission. So, even as APH promotes independence for persons who are blind or visually impaired, the company also impacts the lives of inmates and ex-offenders who learn braille.

CHAPTER NINETEEN

Attending the National Prison Braille Forum and APH Annual Meeting are examples of opportunities I had to network and learn from peers during my years in the field of blindness. I also attended biennial conferences of the Association for Education and Rehabilitation of the Blind and Visually Impaired and meetings held by the American Foundation for the Blind. Though I knew about meetings of the National Braille Association I did not recognize the need to be involved with the group until my focus was on transcribing braille textbooks.

Men in the Braille Program quickly realized I was willing to share information with them when I traveled to professional conferences or received newsletters or journals. I brought back news about products and ideas for improving the books we created in our program. I joined the National Braille Association and passed along copies of the newsletter full of formatting examples. The transcribers also learned the networking I did at these events presented an opportunity for me to invite visitors to our program, educational professionals who could help the men understand more about braille readers and the importance of quality accessible textbooks.

On several occasions we welcomed staff from the American Printing House for the Blind to our prison. The APH visitors knew, perhaps better than most, the importance of our work and the potential employment options for transcribers. They offered training to help ensure transcribers produced braille textbooks that met the company's high standards. The staff from APH presented information about creating tactile graphics and formatting guidelines. When it came time to evaluate members of our group who studied an in-house course on textbook formatting, APH staff accepted an invitation to participate in a special event.

Long-time program veteran Roger Deaton developed an in-house course to prepare transcribers for the important certification test conducted by the

National Braille Association. Knowing the learning styles of his fellow inmates, Roger had collaborated with *Chad Pool* to create games to test skills throughout the course. They prepared a grand finale competition to wrap things up, and we asked the APH staff to serve as judges. The visitors noted whether or not an individual answered correctly, explained some important issues as the competition progressed, and the comprehensive test became a learning opportunity for all the program participants even if they were not directly involved in the course.

Before our APH visitors left, they asked to share the game format and test questions with others in the field - not simply other prison braille programs, but other transcribing groups. The prison's warden, who had been present for the competition, saw the value of networking with APH, heard their discussion about the importance of quality braille programs and their graduates, and he heard their impressions of the work being done by our group, the Georgia Braille Transcribers

The training APH provided was important, but so was the message of support their presence sent to prison officials. For instance, when Nancy Lacewell, Director of Government and Community Affairs at APH, attended the Braille Program Open House in 2007, she was able to discuss the impact of braille programs nationwide. She told corrections officials about employment opportunities for ex-offenders who were well trained in braille and shared data from the National Prison Braille Network that suggested an almost-zero recidivism rate for men and women who participated in prison braille programs.

We had other important visitors from the field of blindness, too. Each year, the men looked forward to meeting a handful of Georgia Teachers of the Visually Impaired (TVI). More than a hundred TVIs came to Macon for an annual conference, and a small group was allowed to select a tour of the program as one activity during their three day conference. The transcribers recognized Georgia TVIs were their primary customers so they took the opportunity to gather feedback on textbooks previously done and seek answers to questions that would help create better textbooks in the future.

A favorite visitor was Dr. Frances Mary D'Andrea, a national expert on braille literacy. Dr. D'Andrea and I had known each other since her days as an itinerant TVI in Georgia and when she worked at the Atlanta office of the American Foundation for the Blind. I usually referred to my friend as FM, and after she received her doctorate in education, many of our colleagues called her Dr. FM. When Frances Mary let me know she was coming to Macon to conduct training at the Georgia Academy for the Blind, I asked if she would carve out some time to speak to the transcribers in our program.

A few of the men were in awe when they recognized Dr. D'Andrea was the author of a major publication on braille literacy and had steered the organization's National Braille Literacy program when she worked for AFB. Protocol dictated I introduce our guest by her title, but the men were delighted when our guest insisted it was okay for them to call her Dr. FM. They were even more pleased by her presentation about the importance of quality accessible materials for students learning to read braille, her openness to answering questions about braille and literacy, and her great interest in demonstrations of their work.

I hope the practice of having such visitors from the field of blindness helped lay a foundation for men in Georgia Braille Transcribers to aspire to greater levels of professionalism. I certainly witnessed their efforts to do so during events such as our annual Open House.

Each year, the Georgia Braille Transcribers hosted an Open House to bring in education and corrections officials to view their work and get a better understanding of our goals to produce quality braille textbooks. The men created posters and prepared demonstrations about the manual braille writer, the course of study, the computerized braille embosser, tactile graphics, and more. Nancy Lacewell and others were impressed at the inaugural Open House by how each man handled his part of the program, and we enjoyed a running joke each year about who would be assigned to guard the food. (During the first Open House, since our two newest program participants had not completed even the first lesson in the course, they served as hosts. A very nervous *John Jeffries* stood at attention near the refreshment table, and his fellow inmates decided John was an effective guard since there was lots of food left over for them after the guests departed.) My favorite memory from the very first Open House, though, was a comment from the Deputy Warden who served as our administrative contact within the prison - "These men really know what they're doing!"

Each subsequent Open House brought more elaborate displays as the men grew in confidence. Yes, they "really knew what they were doing," and certainly, they knew more braille than most visitors who attended, but the men also did copious research to prepare themselves. They asked me to find information about blind musicians to include on a poster about music braille, and they created a cardboard replica of a guitar to demonstrate how to read musical notations in braille. Men prepared a tactile image of the Georgia Braille Transcribers logo and added a special braille message to hand out to visitors as a souvenir. Others in the group prepared a demonstration for the complete process from scanning and translating a textbook all the way through to producing it in hard-copy braille for the student. They stacked the twenty volumes required for one braille book alongside its print counterpart to provide a visual comparison of the two versions. Our assignments coordinator highlighted data on the number of textbooks we transcribed during the previous year, and we posted data on the amount of money saved because our program provided newly transcribed textbooks that the Georgia Department of Education did not have to purchase from an outside vendor. We sometimes had coverage on local television stations or in the local newspaper so the general public could also see a positive side of men behind bars.

The annual Open House was a way to provide a glimpse of the professionalism men developed in the Braille Program. Visitors from the Georgia Department of Education, Teachers of the Visually Impaired, and the Printing House helped send a message to prison officials about the impact our program had on braille readers. And, the corrections officials and members of the Parole Board who attended Open House saw inmates doing good work and demonstrating a determination to carry their program success into other areas of their lives.

During Open House, my colleague Bill Hinton and I stood like proud parents as visitors observed the professionalism we saw on a daily basis. We knew men in the Braille Program set goals for braille production; they monitored the progress of textbook projects to ensure a book was not delayed unnecessarily; they looked for ways to keep learning, improving, and sharing their knowledge.

One example of their efforts to constantly improve skills was the effort transcribers made to clarify textbook formatting. They wanted to be sure the entire team worked with the best answers available when a question arose about correct formatting. As a member of the National Braille Association (NBA), I could post questions to an on-line forum called *Ask An Expert*. One day when Ethan Myers asked me to check for a reply to a recent question, I stumbled on data that indicated our group was one of the top users of Ask An Expert.

It was not enough for the transcribers to simply ask the experts, review the answer, and go about their business. Steven Garmin, Ethan Myers, and Roger Deaton usually asked me to print questions and answers - not just our posts, but those of other site users as well - so they could catalog the information into a file that would be useful to all the transcribers. The three worked with another member of the group to create a searchable database of the information so a transcriber could quickly find a relevant reference.

Steven, Roger, and others also helped me develop a resource packet transcribers could use as they transitioned out of prison. We wanted the packet to contain easily accessible information to help the men as they became independent transcribers without the familiar team inside the fence readily available to help. They understood the information was readily available outside, though not always readily accessible, and they wanted fellow transcribers to get accustomed to looking for answers on their own, checking various resources to ensure they created the best braille possible. (We tried to provide the information on a flash drive when a transcriber transitioned out but sometimes problems arose. Technology advances since I left the program now allow for an inmate's resource files to be dropped into an account on the cloud so he can retrieve them once he has access to the internet.)

As the program matured, I learned it was not only the veterans who approached their work with a sense of pride and professionalism. Chad Pool, a relative newcomer in the Braille Program, came to me with a proposal to develop a computerized version of the *Braille Enthusiast's Dictionary*, a valuable reference for anyone learning braille. The inmate noted how copies of the paperback dictionary - at least the ones he could find since most had disappeared to the dorm or been stashed away in an individual's desk - were falling apart. I knew a similar resource existed on the internet, but inmates did not have access to the online information. I agreed to have Chad proceed with the project as long as it did not interfere with him completing his National Library Services course exercises. He compiled a database with all the words in the braille dictionary, then recruited fellow program participants to help ensure he had them correctly divided into syllables and written correctly in braille. (Chad and his team used "simbraille," a special computer font that shows all six dots of the braille cell with appropriate dots darkened to correspond with a particular braille character.) The completed *eDictionary* allowed the user to type in a word to see the braille view.

Chad's dedication to the *eDictionary* and other aspects of the program reminded me that professionalism did not always translate to enthusiasm for doing braille. He knew the code. He understood the transcription decision process. But, Chad was not fond of transcribing textbooks into braille. As I had often suggested to the men, we considered the idea that an individual who doesn't really like braille might need to move on to something else. Fortunately, the Georgia Instructional Materials Center stepped in with a new project that allowed Chad to redirect his professional spirit to a new task and stay with our program.

Like much of the world today, the field of vision frequently finds itself adapting to new technology. As he prepared the GIMC to address new accessible media issues, Jim Downs observed a relationship between the skills of a braille transcriber and those needed for adapting digital media for classroom use. Chad Pool seized the ideas Jim presented for our new project and quickly became proficient in preparing accessible digital files. With braille, he had learned to scan text and layout braille in a logical linear manner for the reader. He transferred those skills and used his computer background to divide each page into zones and convert the text so an individual could use screen-reading software to move logically through the elements of a textbook page. The transcriber who did not enjoy braille became the leader with digital conversions and coached fellow inmates in tagging text for bookmarks and creating consistent, user-friendly files. Then Chad used the Braille OJT training model to outline a course of study so inmates could earn credits for their work in the new process.

Actions and behaviors such as Chad's, Ethan's, Roger's and Steven's set the standard for how men in the braille program approached their new profession. For instance, Steven Garmin, the long-term veteran of braille who helped guide me in the early days of operating the program, had taught himself how to keep computers running. He relished the challenge of taking apart a non-functioning computer in order to put parts together to get one that worked. But Steven recognized his limits when it came to computer programming, so when we decided to create a massive record-keeping system, he knew we needed help. He recommended *Don Easton* for the program specifically because he knew the inmate had powerful computer programming skills that could help us succeed.

Don entered our program with the understanding he would complete the Braille OJT course of study like everyone else. He submitted braille lessons, then spent hours - in the classroom and in the dorm - creating the database I would use as program administrator and transcribers would use to maintain a record of their work. Don often showed me detailed sketches of a computer screen view, explaining how he envisioned it would work, and he would apologize for taking so long to complete the database. I understood his task was daunting but did not back down on the requirement he earn his Braille OJT certificate. I was pleased to see Don earn the OJT certificate from a local technology school, as well as his literary braille transcribing certificate, and complete the valuable database before I left the program. I was further impressed to see the database in use when I visited during Open House in 2013. The professional product was worth the time he spent, and I feel the braille studies might have helped him better understand the needs of transcribers as he developed something they could use to maintain records of their work and track the progress of textbook assignments.

Another product that was well worth the wait came after I left the program in 2012. Ethan Myers, the transcriber who best understood the special Nemeth code for math and science, researched new rules and information in *Guidelines and Standards for Tactile Graphics 2010.* The publication from the Braille Authority of North America (BANA) delineated how transcribers should prepare tactile images in order to offer a consistent style in math and science textbooks. Ethan prepared a workbook and created a course to assist transcribers in their independent study of the BANA guidelines. As they proceeded through the guidelines, Ethan's course of study provided exercises so the transcriber could test his understanding of the complex material. Ethan and I felt his explanations about how national guidelines helped a tactile graphics designer prepare textbooks might help teachers as they worked with students, so I took great pride in showing Ethan's *Introduction to Mathematical Diagrams: Applying the Guideline and Standards for Tactile Graphics, 2010* to Georgia Teachers of the Visually Impaired during their annual conference in 2013. With his permission, I also shared a copy with a nationally renowned TVI whose work focused on math. The expert applauded Ethan's effort and noted the critical importance of quality Nemeth braille.

Ethan modeled some of his work with the tactile graphics course on Roger Deaton's effort from 2011. Roger, who attained his National Braille Association formatting certificate, lobbied for me to add the important training to our curriculum. I reminded Roger my certification was limited to literary braille transcribing and I did not have a sufficient background in formatting to create such a course. Roger assured me he could plan the course, and he volunteered to prepare all the materials and deliver the training.

As it had been when I trusted Steven Garmin to introduce new students to the basics of braille, I turned over the textbook formatting course idea to Roger. Together, we selected a group of transcribers who expressed an interest in the course; Roger organized class discussions, then provided instruction and support as the men went through the course. I secured copies of the course materials and workbook Roger developed, maintained a presence during sessions, monitored student progress, and sat in for the periodic exams that were presented in the form of a game. I was especially impressed to realize Roger - who was scheduled to be paroled within the next year - took the initiative to groom Joshua Walker so he could take over the training in subsequent offerings of the course. Roger and his protege Joshua were hesitant about their ability to "teach" the course but appreciated the experience and I saw their confidence and skills grow as they proceeded through the task.

Perhaps approval of such activities gave men in the Braille Program the confidence to ask for their own professional development conference. They had devoured handouts and information I brought from conferences, as well as information I downloaded from the California Transcribers and Educators for the Visually Impaired or the National Braille Association training events. I remembered what Jim Downs said when he recruited me to the Braille Program - these men knew more braille than I would ever know - so I turned to them to determine which topics to offer.

A leadership team planned the event, lining up concurrent sessions like they had seen in my conference schedules. They identified topics such as specific textbook formatting issues, tactile graphics guidelines, basic computer repair, and braillewriter repair. The planning team also understood the value of fun during a conference, so they scheduled a competition to see who was the fastest, most efficient braillist when using manual braillewriters. They considered refreshments, so during the weeks prior to the workshop, those who could donated food. A spot in my office filled up with packets of tortillas, tuna, and other items inmates could purchase in the commissary. The appointed chef checked the supply and planned meals of tuna casserole and burritos to serve everyone during the workshop. For my part, I asked the Deputy Warden about having popcorn for one of the breaks during the workshop. I also asked the planning committee to reserve time for a general session for which I would invite a keynote presenter.

I actually invited two presenters. TVI Mary Fitch was a colleague from my days at the Georgia Academy for the Blind, she was from the area, and her former student was enrolled in a local college. Dustin, who was blind from a very early age, grew up learning to read braille, and I felt it would be helpful to have him discuss hurdles he overcame because of his blindness, how he balanced interdependence with independence, and how he made his way in the world in spite of difficulties presented by his disability. I asked Mary and Dustin to comment on the importance of quality braille and hoped the visit with a successful young braille reader would inspire the transcribers. An added bonus was finding out the young man had been a champion in the state Braille Challenge, an event similar to the competition the men planned for their entertainment during the workshop.

The inaugural Georgia Braille Transcribers Professional Development Workshop came about because of the commitment of professionals inside the prison. It proved to be a success because of men who were confident in their skills and some who gained confidence as they met the challenge of presenting to others.

When I look back on that special day, I'm not sure what I enjoyed most: watching quiet *Ken Brown* challenge his audience to figure out what two pieces of 100 or more were missing from a braillewriter he had disassembled and spread on the table, much like Steven Garmin's session on troubleshooting computers; seeing the level of detail in Ethan Myer's presentation on Nemeth Code or Roger Deaton's session on textbook formatting; observing *Tommy Griffin* while he demonstrated strategies for creating tactile graphics; Chad Pool guiding peers through the steps of creating a digital conversion of a textbook; Joshua Walker referring to American Printing House for the Blind staff as he discussed the importance of preliminary pages; or any of the dozen other sessions offered during the two-day event. And, much like the excitement I wanted to bring back to the prison from conferences I attended, I wanted to share with others the accomplishments these men had demonstrated on the inside. Skills. Confidence. Professionalism.

CHAPTER TWENTY

Perhaps Henry Ford was right about professional spirit. He suggested individuals seek professional integrity from pride, not from compulsion. But, what is the source of such pride? How do men who live institutional lives learn to ignore negative influences all around them and focus on moving in a positive direction? Why did men in the Braille Program decide to keep at their work?

Bill Hinton and I directed a program that offered inmates new skills and an opportunity to boost their self-esteem. Beyond that, though, we gave them little other than our respect and guidance. Georgia did not credit inmates with "good time" to reduce the length of their sentences, and income generated from the Braille Program went back into supplies and materials - not to inmates. So what kept the men motivated to spend hours a day preparing quality braille textbooks?

I know some of the men appreciated an opportunity to serve as leaders and perhaps were motivated from being a positive role model. A few recognized the benefits of simply gaining new skills and accepting responsibilities as part of life-long learning. Certainly, some men took solace in being part of a program that offered an escape from the dorm in a relatively quiet place. Regardless of their reasons, it seemed most of the program participants thoroughly enjoyed the challenge of learning braille, and I saw many set a goal for themselves to become the best transcriber possible.

Bill and I did what we could to support those goals, especially because we knew the national reputation for transcribers leaving prison braille programs. Those who dedicated themselves to study as much as possible and attain advanced levels of certification would have a decent chance to find braille work when they left prison; and more certificates improved their chances. We also recognized that completing work assignments helped an inmate build a portfolio he could use to highlight his skills for future employers.

I hope our support and encouragement to help them prepare for their future provided some motivation for men to do well in the Braille Program. My own motivation for coordinating the Braille Program started with meeting the needs of students who read braille. It grew to include the idea that our vocational program would help inmates as they transitioned back into society.

If the focus on positive work ethics and taking pride in a job well done helped prepare all of the men for work when they left prison, then I am satisfied with the work I did.

CHAPTER TWENTY-ONE

When people learn I worked in a prison, they sometimes ask if I ever felt threatened. The answer is, "Not really."

For the most part, my experiences with inmates were positive and non-threatening. I felt safe around the men in the Braille Program, and generally around other inmates as well. Still, I always tried to keep Officer Foston's advice in mind - remember where you work.

One exception to my comfort among inmates in the program came with Dave Lawson, one of the ten men assigned to start with me at Scott State Prison. Dave was a large imposing man who, like some other very intelligent individuals I knew, had little regard for the opinions of others he deemed to be less intelligent. He was very quick to express his frustration with others, and I was a bit intimidated, especially considering his life sentence. I understood Dave Lawson had most likely taken at least one life before being incarcerated some thirty-five years before I met him.

Dave's intelligence served him well as he accepted the challenges of learning braille, including his first opportunity to operate a computer. He was not so ready to accept my role as program coordinator and how I deferred to another inmate for advice specific to braille. He let it be known he was not happy about taking criticism from the certified braille transcriber who graded his lessons, and even after earning his certificate, Dave intimidated fellow transcribers and proofreaders who tried to suggest corrections on his braille projects. Often, Dave simply ignored the advice of more knowledgeable transcribers, and many members of the program refused to work with him. Such behaviors led to a standoff early in our careers together.

Steven Garmin, the lead transcriber who had been certified longer than anyone in the program came to express his frustration at trying to explain to Dave why work he had done was wrong. After listening to Steven's explanation, I decided to discuss the situation with both men. I called them to a conference table to review the textbook issues. We looked at the text in question, the rules for formatting the textbook. I listened to each man's interpretation of the page and the applicable rules. Braille textbook formatting is based on guidelines from the Braille Authority of North America, and unfortunately, the guidelines sometimes suggest it is an "agency decision" on how to address confusing material. I found myself in the position of having to decide which inmate's interpretation would determine our agency's decision. When I chose the more veteran transcriber's opinion over Dave's, he suggested I was "micromanaging" and needed to leave my nose out of inmates' business. I took a deep breath and informed Dave it was my job to know their business as it pertained to the Braille Program. Then, I gave the inmate a choice to follow through as directed or return to the dorm.

Dave Lawson seemed to think I was removing him from the Braille Program altogether rather than suggesting he leave for a while to cool off. I explained my purpose for the ultimatum and made it clear I was not planning to issue a disciplinary report (DR) because of the situation.

"BUT," I assured him, "I will write you up if it becomes necessary!"

Dave returned to his desk to stew and supposedly correct the braille work in question. I returned to my office, closed the door, and had a meltdown. I am a crier, so I shed tears to wash away the stress and fear generated by my standoff with Dave. Then, once I calmed down and opened my door, Officer Foston called me to his office.

Inmates and staff often refer to the chain gang rumor mill noting how quickly news travels through a prison. Officer Foston had learned of my incident with Dave Lawson, and he offered to write a DR, escort the inmate out of the program, or take whatever action I felt was needed. I assured the officer I felt the situation had been resolved, but at the end of the day, Officer Foston held Dave back to remind him of the rules for staying in the Braille Program. Dave resented the officer's reprimand, but I think he must have appreciated that my response to our confrontation was not more punitive. (Ironically, soon after our confrontation, Dave ended up in "the hole" for a different situation. According to the DR, an inmate from another vocational program swung first after blocking the doorway to our program area, and Dave had responded in kind. The DR court - prison officials who review evidence and statements - determined Dave was clear to return to the Braille Program where he continued to work the rest of his time in prison.) It took time, but I think Dave came to understand my focus was on making the Braille Program the best possible experience for everyone involved.

Though he never again directed his anger or frustration at me, Dave continued to present a challenge to the program. Other transcribers often asked to not be assigned on a team with him, and they sometimes went behind him to correct work before it was sent out to students. Dave recognized his status as a troublemaker, and at the first Open House my husband attended, he proudly introduced himself.

"Oh, you've probably heard about me. I'm Mrs. Amerson's problem child."

Dave and I grew to respect one another through the years, and he put his intimidation skills to work watching out for me as I traveled through the prison. When I announced my pending departure from the Braille Program, Dave congratulated me on my retirement and admitted he would miss me. I realized he and I both had come a long way from our days of micromanager and problem child; we were professional colleagues in the field of braille.

The question of feeling threatened might have been an issue in the presence of inmates from the general population, but I knew security staff was never far away. And, I had a personal security detail of inmates from the Braille Program. I think too, because I tried to treat every inmate with respect, acknowledging their greetings or saying hello as we passed on the walkway, I saw many of the inmates respond in kind. Many stepped aside to allow me to pass, and some apologized if they realized I had overheard them cursing.

Occasionally, though, I distinctly felt the impact of being locked in a facility with 1,000 or more men who had done bad things. For instance, I did not like my early morning arrivals during the winter, and I dreaded the rare times when I had to walk across the compound alone during count periods when inmate traffic was supposed to be limited. At such times, I felt vulnerable.

That feeling of vulnerability returned when I visited the program in a few months after leaving the prison in 2012. The officer assigned to escort me from J-Unit to Administration may have recognized me and thought I was still an employee, so he seemed comfortable stepping back inside the unit to retrieve something before taking me up the hill. I was left standing in the small sally-port outside J-Unit while inmates gathered in the area to return for count. I knew the control officer inside had a camera view and the escort would be back out the door any moment, but I was tense about being surrounded by unfamiliar inmates. Most of the men standing around me were new to Central State Prison and had no idea who I was. Finally, one inmate said hello to me and explained to others, "She used to be the Braille lady." It eased my discomfort, and it seemed the crowd of inmates gave a little more space as we waited for the door to open.

One other incident reminds me of my vulnerability and the sense of potential danger posed by working in a prison. The transcribers had gone up the hill to the dining hall before noon count, and as usual, I tried to block out noise from the dormitories as I enjoyed a quick lunch. Suddenly, I realized the volume and tempo of voices changed; the sergeant shouted extra loud, and other voices rose as officers tried to subdue an unruly inmate. The officers were trying to remove the inmate from the building, and their path meant bringing him past my office. I quickly rose from my desk and closed the door. Locked safely inside, I felt safer as I watched the group struggle past my window to meet CERT team officers who were entering through the building's back door. The unit's sergeant later apologized about the excessive noise and assured me I had not been in any danger. I think, though, he may have appreciated my actions because it meant one less thing to worry about as he and his officers dealt with a volatile situation.

Such disruptions and possible threats were a minor thorn in my experience at the prison. I came to realize most inmates were individuals who had made at least one very bad decision in their lifetime, and I saw - on a daily basis - men who were trying to make positive changes in their lives. As long as I remembered where I worked, paid attention to my surroundings and avoided being taken in by someone's con, as long as I spent my time focused on our work, I had no need to feel threatened.

In the end, fearing my safety was much less a concern than dealing with the angst and hassle of administrative issues which grew to be a major factor in my decision to leave a job I had come to love.

CHAPTER TWENTY-TWO

I came to love the work I did inside a prison and came to have a different perspective on the people held within the confines of its razor-wire boundary. They were men who had done bad things, and I rationalized the reason was related to making at least one very bad decision. For some men, a decision to experiment with drugs or alcohol led to addiction and carried them down a dangerous path. Some young men just wanted to fit in with peers so they decided to do whatever was required to be accepted into a local gang, even if that meant armed robbery or worse. And, for some men and women, a moment of passion they could not, or would not, control changed their lives forever.

I know many colleagues in the Prison Braille Network (and, some in the general public) who understand that. They are willing to put an inmate's past misdeeds in the background while they allow the individual to prove himself or herself. Some people, though, can never put an inmate's criminal actions in the background, and ex-offenders often face prejudice simply because of their records.

Certainly, my impression of inmates was affected by positive experiences I had during my tenure with the Braille Program. But, what if I had ever been the victim of a crime? What if a family member had been harmed by a violent crime? Would I - could I - be willing to expect better of a man if I knew he had hurt someone I loved?

I considered such questions from the perspective of my friend *Emma Cassidy* who was present when her beloved friend opened his front door to a murderer. She knew the man who shot and killed her friend, and during the time before he went to trial, the perpetrator who was out on parole visited Emma's church. On that particular Sunday, Emma was not at church, so her friends relayed the man's message. He wanted to speak to her and explain what happened. Emma chose not to face the man before his trial, and she told me she was pleased he was eventually convicted and sentenced for the crime. She was glad he would pay some price for having taken a father away from his young children.

Yet, Emma also expressed hope she could someday forgive the murderer. She wanted to believe that men in prison who say they have found religion truly understand the power of her Christian faith and realize the pain they caused with their crimes. She was not sure when, or if, she would ever reach the point of forgiving. Years later, though, Emma told me once she recognized that forgiving the man who killed her friend allowed her to move forward in her own life, she was able to sincerely hope prison would help the murderer turn things around for himself.

"It would not be good for a person to go on living like he was when he committed the crime."

Emma's comments help me see that some victims attempt to move on from a crime, going so far as to forgive the perpetrator. But, I've also seen that it is not an easy thing to do, even for families of the inmate.

I remember when one of my teaching friends lay dying of cancer, I sat with others in her home and listened to the phone ring and ring because she refused to let any of us answer. She knew it was her son calling from prison. His substance abuse and actions had created a deep rift in their lives, one she was not willing to address as she took her final breaths. Another family I know refused to post an obituary when the matriarch died because they did not want the son whose drug addiction had broken so many bonds to find a way to use his mother's death as an excuse to leave prison even for a little while.

So, from a distance, I think I understand how victims or families might have difficulty accepting the idea a criminal could change. But, during my time working in prison, I saw many men who became positive influences in the world, men I would accept as having changed from the person who committed an unforgivable sin.

I know there are times when it is not possible or practical to let go of the past. When I first started with the program, I rarely checked the records to note why an inmate was incarcerated, and I never discussed it with the men. Some men told me enough so I understood what crime landed them behind bars, and I came to recognize how fellow inmates interacted differently with men imprisoned for crimes against children. Of course, I also realized men serving a life sentence had probably taken a life. But, the crimes were not my focus.

Eventually, though, Bill and I felt we had to review an inmate's record and consider its impact on his efforts to seek work as a braille transcriber. Many agencies that hire braille transcribers knowing they are ex-offenders try to focus on the individual's current work and not his or her past. But the reality for schools is more sensitive. Education professionals must determine if an ex-offender has a record of crimes against children, even if he or she never comes in contact with students or has his work monitored by other professionals.

Almost every inmate Bill and I interviewed about entering the Braille Program said he wanted to be in the program so he could give back to society. I am naive, but not gullible. I realized many said what they expected I wanted to hear. Yet, I came to realize many were genuine when they expressed regret for their crimes and stated a desire to take positive actions, to make better decisions. As the men learned the complexities of braille, to consider how the reader accessed information or the various guidelines to efficiently transcribe braille textbooks, I saw a shift occur. As transcribers, they *had* to focus on someone else. The men began to realize their stated goal of doing something good for someone else.

So, I had the opportunity to see men in the Braille Program not as criminals. I saw them as men trying to balance their past lives with the life they hoped to lead in the future.

One graduate of the program explained the metamorphoses. In the past, he had always blamed others for his failures. However, he also felt any successes were due to the actions of others as well. Once he overcame the institutional way of life in prison and finally "took ownership" of his life - accepting that his failures and successes were a result of his own actions and reactions - the inmate realized he could be the son and husband and father he wanted to be. He could be a successful member of the community outside the fence.

I've listened to an inmate speak of dreams for his teenage daughter and the hope she would use knowledge of his mistakes as a reminder of risks to avoid in her own life. I watched men grieve for a fellow inmate whose health prompted a transfer to the medical prison before his passing, and a young inmate grieve for the beloved grandmother who raised him, knowing he could not be part of her final goodbye. And, when my mother died, the men not only extended their heartfelt sympathy; they allowed me the peace and quiet I needed to return to the routine of work.

I know families are torn apart by crime, that pain and disappointment often linger. I would never minimize their feelings about the perpetrator of devastating crimes or condemn someone for being unable to forgive. But, I saw the men these inmates had become many years after their crime. I saw empathy, caring, and actions that put others first. I often wished others could see the men as I did and that such a perspective might help survivors reach a point where they could forgive.

I hope, if I were in the victim's shoes, I could.

CHAPTER TWENTY-THREE

Two thousand, two hundred and sixty-seven days after I began my career in the Braille Program, I relinquished my ID and locator cards along with the brass chits embossed with my name and walked away from prison. I had actually been inside the fence only eight hundred and eighteen days during the six years between April 2006 and June 2012. In that time, I came to care deeply about the success of inmates as they learned to transcribe braille textbooks and planned their future lives.

For several months in 2011 and early 2012, my colleague Bill Hinton and I discussed the idea of leaving the program. Bill and his wife were ready to enjoy a true retirement and spend time with their small grandchildren. I was growing more and more frustrated with administrative challenges. So, Bill and I informed Department of Corrections leadership of our plan in an effort to prompt them to lay groundwork for replacing us. We even outlined staffing patterns and offered to help train new staff. Nothing happened. Prison administrators had too many other things on their plate to be concerned about the Braille Program, or perhaps, they thought if they did not create a transition plan we would not leave. Finally, though, we both gave official notice that we would be leaving in June 2012.

Bill and I knew our departure would have a serious impact on the Braille Program, especially as the prison prepared to welcome a new warden on July 1. We also realized we were leaving at a time when the transcribers were swamped with new orders. That was no accident - we felt because their work was so important, the Georgia Instructional Materials Center and the Department of Corrections would find a way to keep the men actively working on braille as they sought staff to replace us.

My decision to leave the Braille Program brought questions that kept me awake at night: How would the program function without the strong advocacy Bill and I had maintained? Would the Braille Program continue to be a valuable source of textbooks for Georgia's students? Would inmates in the program continue to operate as a team and conduct themselves as professionals?

I knew from hearing about other prison braille programs going through change that a key ingredient in their success was the support of prison officials. I took comfort thinking that, except for the new warden, Central State Prison staff knew our program and the reputation of the men as cooperative inmates who rarely caused trouble. The director of Workforce Development who had always been a proponent of a braille program was entrenched within the Department of Corrections, so I hoped she would ensure its future after Bill and I left. I felt, too, the program director for the Georgia Instructional Materials Center would continue to monitor things and communicate with prison officials as needed. He would ensure that students continued to receive the best possible products from Georgia's prison braille program.

I realized some matters I had found frustrating might continue to be an issue for our successors and hoped our replacements would be better prepared than I to deal with administrative red tape. I made the offer to the new warden and other prison officials to provide support for the next program coordinator(s) especially to help answer questions they might have about braille and the field of visual impairments. Bill also made himself available to answer questions about how we had coordinated with others in the Department of Corrections to facilitate transitions and such.

In preparation for leaving, I made copious notes about the program so a new staff member would not have to rely solely on an inmate for the details. I wrote about curriculum and grading, how we processed orders, how we submitted information to a national database so other agencies could order braille textbooks from us. I included a section with action steps Bill and I had used in planning the annual Open House. I highlighted resources in the field who could help answer questions about braille. Since I had always brought in thread from my personal crafting supplies, I considered the next person might not do the same, so I searched for specific ordering information for items the men found most useful for tactile graphics. I left a binder full of notes and information I would have wanted to know when I was starting as a new employee.

One question from my sleepless nights - the one about how men in the program would continue a legacy of professionalism - caused the least concern and lost sleep. I knew the transcribers and digital media specialists would continue to do their best because they took pride in their work. And, though some individuals might shift their team allegiance a bit, I expected the men would always work together to create the best possible products for Georgia's students. That was just who they were.

I left Georgia's prison braille program with the hope it was strong enough and important enough to continue. When Bill and I met the new warden and shared our enthusiasm for the unique program, he listened with great interest, and to my delight, he assigned an officer to be based in the Braille Program's office. She would have other duties, but the officer's presence meant the program could operate while the administration sought replacements for Bill and me. The Workforce Development director secured funding to allow me to contract for a couple of months so I could continue to answer questions about braille, coordinate delivery of textbooks to the instructional materials center, and help ease the transition to a new way of operating the Braille Program.

Inmates who had been program leaders cautiously assumed the same positions under the new structure, making sure they did nothing to alienate the officer assigned to the program. In early August, a new part-time coordinator was hired, followed within a few months by a second part-time employee. The new team provided a similar balance as Bill and I, one with an education background and the other having served as a deputy warden and other corrections positions.

The program operated much as it had in the past with a few exceptions, including personalities of the new leaders. The prison's new warden accepted his deputy's recommendation to move some inmates out of the "braille unit" dormitory. The deputy promoted the idea as a way to place well-behaved inmates into various dorms to serve as role models for the general population, but men in the program felt it was her way of breaking the strong after-hours fellowship of the group. They also saw it as a threat to the quality of their products because they could no longer work and study at night or on weekends in the noisy open dorms. Men in the Braille Program were frustrated about the dormitory assignments, and then they saw a fellow long-time member of the group transferred out with no explanation. Such changes made it difficult for the transcribers to focus on positive steps such as having a popular inmate who had been removed by the previous warden allowed to return and resume his work in the program.

Frustration mounted when questions arose about a long-awaited computer server Bill and I had ordered. During the previous fiscal year, he and I had closely monitored funds generated by our program so we could order equipment to enhance communications and data management within the program. We knew the funds should be sufficient, but the new coordinators had less information about the matter so it took a while to assure the administration it was an appropriate purchase for the Braille Program. Supplies dwindled as deputy wardens - seemingly unaware of the thousands of dollars generated by sales of braille textbooks - also questioned why the Braille Program should be spending more than other vocational programs.

I, too, experienced frustration when I heard of the delays and difficulties the program faced. One especially disappointing incident occurred when a shipment of braille books got destroyed by mistake. My husband worked for the instructional materials center, and when he went to the prison to retrieve braille volumes the men had prepared for Georgia students, the officer at the shake-down shack could not locate any boxes for GIMC. The program coordinator later determined the five boxes of braille volumes (worth at least $2,000) had been put into a truck with other boxes of papers sent out to be shredded.

Men in the Braille Program felt under siege, and morale sank. Even so, the inmates performed their duties and continued to transcribe and produce braille books and digital textbook conversions. They carried on the legacy of professionalism I expected they would. My experiences had taught me that individuals - even inmates - respond in kind to the way they are treated. They appreciate respect and being held accountable to high expectations. I knew men in the Braille Program were professionals who could put others first and complete their work in spite of disruptions and disappointments along the way. They just wanted to feel they and their work were respected.

In prison, though, much as I might wish it not so, most staff look at all inmates as criminals first. I can only hope that wardens, deputy wardens, and other prison staff can learn to balance such a view with the reality that inmates who participate in the Braille Program make a difference in the lives of braille readers as well as in their own lives.

They made a difference in my life, too. I came to understand the true power of respecting one another, and on my last day of work in the Braille Program, I was honored to express appreciation to inmates - for their work, for their commitment, and most of all, for their respect.

EPILOGUE

March, 2013 (Open House)

Twenty-four men, each wearing a white uniform trimmed with a dark blue stripe, turned their attention to a crowd of visitors in suits and business attire. Each man had a role to play. Two introduced visitors to the braille code and its history; another demonstrated a Perkins braillewriter; men showed the process for transcribing textbooks into braille, from the first step of computer translation through formatting and proofreading to production; a poster displayed the fiscal value of the group's work to the state of Georgia; music braille transcribers presented hands-on demonstrations of how a student might use their work; digital media specialists showed how user-friendly the converted files are for visually impaired students. The visitors - people from the Department of Corrections, the Department of Education, Pardons & Paroles, Middle Georgia Technical College, my former co-worker Bill Hinton, and I - viewed the posters and chatted with inmates and observed true professionalism in action.

Nine months after I left my work in prison, I attended the 2013 Georgia Braille Transcribers' Open House. It felt odd to be a guest, but I beamed like a proud mama when other visitors commented on the fine work men in the program were demonstrating. I listened to conversations of men in suits as they talked about evidence of reduced recidivism for inmates who graduated from prison braille programs. I even took it upon myself to help answer a question or two from other guests, almost as if I still coordinated the program.

It seemed clear - even though I left the program in June of 2012 - it would always be a part of me. The professionals in Georgia's prison braille program would always hold a place in my heart.

ABOUT THE AUTHOR

Marie J. Amerson worked with Georgia's prison braille program for more than six years. Before that, she worked at the state's school for students who are blind and learned about the critical importance of quality braille textbooks. Amerson, who long ago learned to teach braille to young students, attained her literary braille transcriber certificate after joining the prison braille program. She never studied for advanced braille certifications, leaving that challenge to the dedicated transcribers in the program.

Amerson served as a member of the writing team for the National Prison Braille Network publication, *Guidelines for Starting and Operating Prison Braille Programs,* © 2009, American Printing House for the Blind.

Amerson has written several books of local interest including the history of an icon in Macon, Georgia - *Remembering Len Berg's Restaurant,* © 2012, Mercer University Press.